Dec. 2019.

Dearest Little Amy

A book combining some
of the things you love —
Christmas... great food...
Floristry... and Downton Abbey!

CHRISTMAS AT HIGHCLERE

RECIPES & TRADITIONS FROM THE REAL DOWNTON ABBEY

Happy Christmas!
All our love,
Mummy and
Daddy

X   X   X

THE COUNTESS OF CARNARVON

For my parents, Ronnie and Frances,
and for Geordie's parents, Henry and Jeanie,
who made Christmas special for all their
children and friends, with laughter,
good food and helping others

CONTENTS

CHRISTMAS AT HIGHCLERE

IS A BOOK ABOUT THE PLANNING AND PARTIES WHICH take place each December at one of the most spectacular houses in England. Highclere Castle enjoys global recognition today through its alter ego, Downton Abbey. It is above all a Victorian home, the period in which the Christmas we know and love today was developed, largely through the influence of Queen Victoria's husband, Prince Albert. From the richness of the interiors, to the traditional meals and gatherings, through to the challenges of decorating a 250-room house, I look at the way my predecessors celebrated and highlight our own traditions today.

There are magnificent state rooms and formal events, cosy family evenings, with charades and sardines, and fabulous New Year's Eve balls, complete with Scottish dancing and bagpipes. One hundred years ago, diaries and letters record the enjoyment of all the household staff when they were allowed their own dance with the staff of other local houses invited as their guests.

Entertaining and cooking have always been at the heart of family life at Highclere Castle. The Estate has always had its own farm and glasshouses on which it depended for much of its produce and this tradition continues today with an emphasis on seasonal, local ingredients. The buildings and architecture may have changed over the centuries, but Highclere has been a home for over 1,000 years. This book delves back in time into our traditions and archives to share how we celebrate at Highclere, what we cook and how we prepare for Christmas.

FIONA - 8TH COUNTESS OF CARNARVON

CHAPTER ONE

CHRISTMAS IS COMING

❦ IT IS LATE SEPTEMBER ❦

AND I CAN FEEL THE LIGHT CHANGING;

THE LOWERING SUN IS WARMING THE EARLY

autumn colours like a slowly developing photograph. We are well

past the longest day of the year. The cycle of the farm, the landscape

and the Castle has begun to find a different gear, as will all those

who work with us on the land, in the gardens and around the house.

I CAN HARDLY BELIEVE THAT, ONCE AGAIN, I AM discussing Christmas trees and decorations and looking towards the end of yet another year. Time is, undoubtedly, relative and the yearly cycles seem to accelerate as my birthdays multiply.

Abbie, who is a new, but remarkably well-named, member of staff, has been assigned the job of ordering Christmas trees for inside the Castle and the doorways, as well as along the driveways and courtyards. With variations of size, spacing and containers taken into account, along with additional requests from Paul the gardener for new containers, the shopping list rapidly grows.

Abbie reports that the proposed Castle Saloon tree should measure twenty-four feet, and whilst I remain silent contemplating that figure, I can hear John Gundill, our Castle Manager, stride into her office saying, with some degree of controlled panic and urgency, that this was definitely too big. In the following three-way conversation, he calls down the phone to me, 'Lady Carnarvon, can you remember what happened last time – it was so wide because of its height that we could not get it through the doors on either side in the Saloon. Say no!'

On consideration, I ask Abbie whether we might not need to find a tree closer to eighteen feet. At twenty-four feet the tree would effectively be a man's height taller. Just imagine a whole John on top of the Christmas tree – it would be far too much – and I think Sally from the gift shop would prefer the fairy or angel option...

Sally tends to be in charge of Christmas at the Castle. Quite early on in the year she and I sit down with the obligatory cappuccino to discuss the themes for this year's tree and decorations. Once agreed, it then becomes her project, and we all more or less fall into line to become her Christmas elves. In a Castle tradition, borrowed from the film of *Bridget Jones's Diary*, everyone involved in raising the Saloon Christmas tree has to wear a suitably festive and 'sillier-the-better' Christmas sweater. Competition is always keen, and I think our collective efforts for ridiculous jumpers have long since exceeded those from the film, with the winner, more often than not, being Paul McTaggart, our security officer.

THE CASTLE NEVER USED TO BE OPEN AT ALL IN December. In fact, we began opening almost by accident by offering to hold an event – a fair to raise money for our local Air Ambulance. This must be some twelve years ago now, and the fair remains one of my favourite winter events that we have held at the Castle. The fair now always takes place in the first week of December, on the principle that it is a good time to begin to celebrate Christmas. Any earlier and it is just too hard to contemplate! We invite various local trades and craftspeople to join with us to sell myriad items from homewares, hats and jewellery to decorations, food and wine. Our kitchen team fills the tearooms with mince pies, hot

TOP
Highclere's Saloon welcomes
a festive party

BOTTOM
The dining room table set for
feasting

TOP
Carols at Christmas
BOTTOM
Christmas lunch with all the
trimmings

soups and Christmas quiches, whilst local choirs and bands get us into the festive spirit with carols and music to accompany visitors from stall to stall. We run the fair over two days, with the opening one extending into the evening for those not able to come during the daytime. I've heard that men in particular have been known to spend ridiculous sums of money on Christmas Eve, madly panic-buying presents because Christmas has, once again, caught them by surprise, so I hope that our evening opening provides a convivial and effortless way for them to buy a range of presents that their loved ones might actually want.

I have myself been on the receiving end of a last-minute, if well-intentioned, gift when Geordie staggered in one Christmas morning bearing something that seemed deliciously heavy for me to open. Excited and mystified, I unwrapped a large, marble pestle and mortar. Lost for words, I looked at my husband, who explained into the silence that on Christmas Eve the only department in Harrods that was not a terrible crush was kitchenwares. Since then he has, wisely, avoided purchasing presents from kitchen departments.

HOWEVER, COOKING, AND THE KITCHEN, IS IN MANY ways the essence of Christmas. This book is a journey through the festive season at Highclere, both past and present – through food, feasting and celebrations. Winter foods are the fruits and cuts of meat which we gain from the 'wanton burthen' of the 'teeming autumn' *(Sonnet 97,* William Shakespeare) and are at the centre of our celebrations, both formal and informal.

Family and friends gather together to share food and gifts, to toast the year past and look forward to new beginnings. It is the time when almost everyone in the world stops, and it is the time when we contemplate and celebrate with those dearest to us the precious gifts of life, love and the hope for a fulfilling and happy new year.

At its heart, Christmas Day is, of course, a Christian religious festival, but today it is observed as a major celebration and public holiday in countries around the world by both Christians and non-Christians alike. In some countries it has simply become incorporated into the calendar through global cultural influences, which has led to many of the more secular aspects of Christmas, such as gift-giving, decorations and Christmas trees, being enthusiastically adopted.

Christmas at Highclere combines both ancient rituals bearing witness to centuries of traditions and more modern customs culled from my own family. Combined with the beauty of the land surrounding us, it provides a heritage that makes Christmas here uniquely special.

CHAPTER TWO

PLANNING & PREPARATION

❈ COME OCTOBER, IT IS ❈
A GOOD IDEA TO START THINKING ABOUT

LIST-MAKING, SO THAT AS 'ACTUAL' CHRISTMAS approaches the whole thing is less stressful. As a student I always thought planning ahead was anathema and would make me seem old; today, ironically, I find it difficult to operate without dates, lists and order.

PART OF THE ESSENCE OF CHRISTMAS IS A LITTLE BIT of old-fashioned magic, but to create it and, even more so, to be able to enjoy it yourself, you need paper and a pen. 'Planning is everything', as Dwight D. Eisenhower wisely commented. I do agree...

My immediate action today is coffee and 'let's find Sally in the gift shop'. Purpose restored, I walk through the stables, glancing at the immaculate straw beds all ready for lucky horses, and pull back the heavy sliding door leading into the gift shop area. Sally is staring intently at her computer screen, surrounded by piles of papers, giving John Gundill a run for his money. (He is renowned for papers, files and filing cupboards, but she comes a close second.) Keen for a walk, we decide the Castle tearooms and a coffee will inspire the lists.

A multiple number of layers of thought and planning are needed at Highclere all year round, but it is particularly true at Christmas, as the Castle will be open to welcome visitors and guests, as well as family and friends, over much of the festive season. Inspiration often comes from books but also from the magical landscape that surrounds us. I grew up with my head in books, reading several at once, and continue to do so. There are piles of books everywhere: by beds, by desks and in baskets propped on chairs. Then, of course, there is the Library itself, such a beautifully proportioned crimson and gilded room. With over 6,500 books lining its shelves, it contains a wealth of stories about people and places.

ABOVE
Christmas lights illuminate the
books in the North Library

ABOVE RIGHT
An extract from a 19th-century
Christmas gift list at Highclere

14

DATE.	NAME.	PARISH.	WHAT GIVEN.	REMARKS.

DATE.	NAME.	PARISH.	WHAT GIVEN.	REMARKS.

Christmas is all about stories: listening to them, watching them and hearing them. They open up magical worlds for your eyes to wonder at, reveal things to feel scared of for a moment, or distant lands not yet visited, tales of ballets and theatres to visit, fantastically decorated fairy tales – the Nutcracker, the Snow Queen, and of course the story of Christmas itself.

There are plenty of practical tasks to be done as well. I already have a basket for collecting wrapping paper and ribbons, and have even bought a few early presents. I feel it is less of a budgetary blow if the purchasing of such things is spread out over several weeks, or even months. I always try to give some small presents to the team who help us here, and then, of course, there are family, close friends, godchildren, guests and various others whom I have undoubtedly forgotten.

I found a Christmas present list from the end of the nineteenth century filed in the archives, everything neatly noted down, and it was so reassuring that nothing really changes and the numbers remain rather immense. I do mean to do Christmas cards, too, and every year I start with good intentions, but at the thought of this, by now I need a second cup of coffee.

Sally has various alter egos, of which just one is Chief Christmas Elf, when she supervises the master list to check against all other elves' lists. The usual starting point is testing the Christmas tree lights and batteries. She will also delegate to an elf who doesn't mind stairs and dark corridors the job of discovering the whereabouts of the various boxes of ornaments

LIST-MAKING

I would recommend using the following headings:

FOOD

WINE AND SPIRITS

GIFTS

STOCKINGS

CHRISTMAS CARDS

EVENTS

GUESTS

ALL OTHER ITEMS

A more modern pottage
and an excellent soup
for lunch whilst you are
doing your planning:
WHITE ONION
AND TRUFFLE SOUP
PAGE 22

and decorations we have here, so she at least knows where they are. It is always very annoying when a non-Christmas elf helpfully moves them to a new place for some good, but undocumented, reason, then fails to tell anyone.

I have a large notebook which I am shortly likely to lose, but in the meantime I write a list for Christmas stockings, some general headings for a list of cards, and again for a list of presents. Sally has a larger notebook in which she keeps a list of all the various tasks that need to be performed, and by whom. Our Events Managers Stephanie and Charlotte have bulging files containing details of all the various events that are happening, whilst Paul, our head chef, prefers obsessively organised computer lists and schedules.

Such planning has not always been this light-hearted at Highclere; in the past, actually making sure you survived the winter dominated the estate's schedule. Storing food for this barren season and deciding which of the animals to slaughter to help the community survive were vital issues. Advent was a time of fasting, as most families would limit much of their eating until the great day of Christmas itself.

Good crop choice was essential at sowing time; beans and peasecods were grown and carefully dried as a source of both food and animal fodder over winter. Pottage – a thick soup or stew – was a staple of the peasant diet, and a pot of it was generally kept cooking at all times, topped up with new ingredients as required. An old English nursery rhyme is not far off the mark: 'Pease pudding hot, pease pudding cold – Pease pudding in the pot, nine days old'.

'Bere', meaning barley, was an ancient grain brought to Britain by the Vikings, which became an important multi-use crop – for malting to become beer, milling to become food and as thatching for crofts. The enormous medieval barn we still have here on the farm testifies to the central role that this grain played in the processing of such a key crop over six hundred years ago.

FASTING AND FEASTING
CHRISTMAS AT HIGHCLERE IN 1400 AD & THE GREAT BARN

IN THE YEARS BEFORE 1400, THE HARVESTS AT HIGHCLERE had been good and the Bishop of Winchester, William of Wykeham, had used some of the proceeds to repair the barn at Old Burghclere, not far from the Castle.

Craftsmen drawn from other Winchester manors had spent the summer rebuilding the bays to such great proportions and height that the barn now seemed more like a cathedral. Fresh timber had been supplied, but where possible the original purlins, or beams, were reused. Taking no chances,

the craftsmen had drawn two witch's marks – one by the great door of the barn and one at the back – to ward off evil spirits.

In the barn, grain would be threshed, sifted and then hung in bundles from the rafters. It should last for a year if kept dry and free from vermin, but this was not always easy. Some of the wheat was milled and taken back to be stored in individual workers' homes, but as flour has a much shorter shelf-life, milling the grain was generally done as and when necessary.

The harvest of 1400 AD had also been good and by late autumn the reeve, a local official, had already discussed which animals to slaughter, as they couldn't feed them all through the winter. The Bishop had been generous and directed that Palace staff and clergy would receive two carcasses of beef, two of venison, three calves, pigs, fowls, partridges and geese, as well as bread and cheese. There would be thirty gallons of red wine, another four gallons of white and plenty of beer, whilst the older hens and pigs would be culled. It would be a good feast this Christmas. Any offal and leftovers would then be mixed with vegetables to make a hearty pie – a 'humble pie'.

Every man at Highclere was given a loaf of bread and a dish of meat on Christmas Eve, whilst his dog would get a loaf on Christmas Day. Another three tenants on the same manor would share two loaves of bread, an 80lb 'mess' of salt beef, a side of bacon with mustard, one chicken, some cheese, fuel for cooking and as much beer as they could drink during the day.

The dark-sided dwellings where the men lived lay in the lee of the

prevailing wind and weather, below the main manor buildings but not too far from the water well. Following the deaths and devastation of the plague years, Bishop William was more generous with the timber from Highclere than he had been for his customary tenants. The reeve had let the tenants harvest some strong trees to shape and rebuild the three arched bays which formed the frame for each house, before the walls were filled in with wood and thatch, leaving a smoke louvre in the middle of the roof over the hearth.

By this point in history, the Bishops of Winchester had owned Highclere for nearly 650 years, but rather than building an abbey, William of Wykeham had constructed a palace with two courtyards, a bakery, gardens, dovecote, orchards, fishponds and a grange on the same site as the previous, more ramshackle, collection of buildings. Behind the palace there were also storerooms, stables, pasture land, a deer park and many sheep. Wykeham had a growing reputation for the supervision and administration of royal building works, especially during the reign of Edward III, and he became a powerful financial administrator of many royal castles and manors. Highclere had recently been a centre of church development, and was a house to which William of Wykeham often retired to rest and conduct business. As such it played host to a great many people and was therefore in constant need of maintenance and repair. In this point, little has changed over the centuries.

ABOVE
Sheep safely graze on the
Highclere Estate; a scene that
has not changed for centuries

18

CHRISTMAS CARDS
& GETTING AHEAD WITH THE COOKING

IN THE MEANTIME, IN A MORE MODERN AGE, I KNOW that November is the month when I need to begin to write the Christmas cards, discuss foliage and winter plants with the gardening team, consult with Head Chef Paul and his kitchen team over menus and various food requirements, understand which choirs we have asked to support us, and fill the diary with a raft of future meetings. On the home front, at this time Geordie meets with our butler Luis to review what is in the cellars and which wines might be served on the bigger, more elaborate evenings for our family and friends.

IN BROWN ARCHIVE BOXES STORED IN THE LEATHER-lined archive room two floors above my study, I once found a large brown box with manila files inside. Along with letters and sketches, there were bundles of Christmas cards tied up with ribbon, each decorated with plump robins on holly branches, wreaths of mistletoe, snowy scenes with children and coachmen with well-fed gleaming horses carrying laughing passengers through the snow. Personally, I suspect travel by coach was in reality both exceedingly uncomfortable and probably rather cold.

Elizabeth, 4th Countess of Carnarvon, had carefully kept these treasures. Pregnant with her second child, who was due sometime in December 1882, before the New Year, Elizabeth was looking forward to Christmas. I wonder if she read these cards, and wrote her own, in the same sitting room that I use, or perhaps at a desk by the fire in the Saloon; fountain pen, ink, blotter and cards to hand whilst she made a careful record of which friends had written to her. Moments like these are the quiet ones in my day; admiring the sketches of birds and churches on the cards, reminders of far-flung family and friends.

ABOVE
Victorian Christmas cards
from the archive

19

By the latter half of the nineteenth century the idea of sending little cards by post had become a big business. Christmas cards were invented by Sir Henry Cole a few years after the Penny Post was introduced in 1840, and forty years later posting letters and cards had become affordable for a much larger number of people. Cole had become very successful, too, so it was rather sad that he had just died at that time.

Picking up the cards on the piano in the Drawing Room today, there are still robins, coachmen, drawings of stars and charming thatched village houses covered in snow, demonstrating how the more traditional styles of Christmas card design have not changed much over the years.

These days Geordie and I tend to use a different view of the Castle each year on our cards, some fun sketches from Victorian times, or a dog or two in the snow. One autumn, however, I had asked about twelve girlfriends to come to stay and have supper as a treat for my birthday. Towards the end of the evening, Geordie gate-crashed and we had the impulsive idea he should sit on the footstool in the Library whilst my girlfriends draped themselves around him, as a memento of the evening. It became a memorable Christmas card that was sent to a few of our friends.

The postal service has been part of our lives for the last 150 years but today quite a few cards arrive by email. You open them, and a few minutes later they are gone. Whilst diverse communication may be advantageous, and I try to not be a stick in the mud, I can't help but think how much nicer and more touching it is to hold something tangible sent by a friend and read their handwritten words.

LATE NOVEMBER IS ALSO A GOOD TIME TO BEGIN preparing the festive feast. Some of the Christmas cooking can not only be done in advance but positively needs to be prepared ahead, in order for the flavours to mature. This includes the Christmas cake and pudding, chutneys, pickles and flavoured spirits, which are not only warming to drink but make excellent gifts as well.

Some recipes to help
you get ahead:
SLOE GIN
PAGE 24
CHRISTMAS CAKE
PAGE 26
SPICED BEETROOT
CHUTNEY
PAGE 33

WHITE ONION AND TRUFFLE SOUP

This soup is very much a favourite of my son Edward. It is very pretty and pale, but the truffle oil enhances its flavour. If you can, look for the proper oil – you don't need much, you are just adding it at the very end.

PREPARATION TIME 10 mins   COOKING TIME 35 mins   SERVES 6–8

INGREDIENTS

100g (3½oz)
    unsalted butter
4 large onions, sliced
3 celery stalks, chopped
1 leek (white part only),
    sliced
1 litre (1¾ pints)
    vegetable stock
2 bay leaves
5 garlic cloves, thinly sliced
5 sprigs of thyme
300ml (10fl oz) double
    cream
Salt and pepper
Truffle oil, to serve

METHOD

§   Melt the butter in a heavy-based pan over a medium heat. Add the onions, celery and white part of the leek and sweat for 5 minutes, stirring often until softened but not coloured. Add the vegetable stock, bay leaves, garlic and thyme. Bring it up to the boil and simmer for 20 minutes.

§   Blitz with a stick blender until completely smooth. Stir in the cream and season to taste. Return to the heat and simmer for a further 10 minutes or until it reaches your preferred thickness. If the soup is too thick, add a little more cream.

§   To serve, drizzle each bowl of soup with a little truffle oil. We don't pass the soup, but you can if you prefer.

SLOE GIN

Sloes (the fruit of the blackthorn) grow wild all around the Highclere Estate. This recipe requires no cooking, just patience while you wait for the delicious, amethyst liquor to steep. If you can't find sloes, blackberries make a good alternative, although the resulting drink will be much sweeter. This makes a wonderful winter warmer for one's hipflask or else a deliciously sour long drink topped up with tonic water.

INGREDIENTS

500g (1lb 2oz) sloes
200g (7oz) sugar
1 bottle of Highclere
    Castle Gin

METHOD

§   Prepare the sloes (see tip below), then add them to a large, airtight jar with the sugar and the gin. Seal the jar and set in a cool, dry place. Shake the jar every day for the first week, then shake once a week for at least 2 months.

§   After this time, strain the sloes through a sieve, then through muslin and pour the liquid into sterilised bottles (see page 308). For an even clearer finish, strain through a coffee filter.

[CHEF'S TIP: Traditionalists say one should begin by pricking the sloes all over with a darning needle so as to break their tough skins. However, I have found that by leaving them in the freezer overnight and then defrosting them, this breaks down the skins perfectly.]

CHRISTMAS CAKE

There is no clear history to the Christmas cake, it seems quite similar to the Christmas pudding (see page 57) and, like the pudding, can hold its own for a good number of days. It is always there to welcome any teatime guests. It has a lengthy ingredient list and when it is offered at teatime someone likes the icing, another does not like the marzipan (me), but I love the inside stickiness of the fruit cake part.

This is Paul's recipe, whereas I might add some prunes or figs as well.

I also make it a week or two before I need it and keep it moist with a regular supply of brandy. You need to pierce the bottom of the cake with a skewer and carefully pour over 3–4 tablespoons and repeat every four or five days. Wrap it in baking paper and cling film and store it in an airtight tin at the back of the pantry.

PREPARATION TIME 3 days   COOKING TIME 4 hours minimum (maybe 5)   SERVES 8–12

INGREDIENTS

350g (12oz) currants
225g (8oz) sultanas
225g (8oz) raisins
75g (3oz) glacé cherries, chopped
4 tbsp brandy, plus extra for keeping it moist
250g (9oz) plain flour
Pinch of salt
Pinch of grated nutmeg
Pinch of mixed spice
250g (9oz) soft brown sugar
250g (9oz) unsalted butter
4 eggs, beaten
50g (2oz) almonds
75g (3oz) candied peel
Zest of 1 lemon
Zest of 1 large orange
2 tbsp black treacle

METHOD

§   The day before baking, mix all the fruits with the brandy in a bowl, cover and leave overnight to absorb the liquid.

§   The next day, preheat the oven to 140°C/275°F/Gas mark 1 and grease and line a 17cm (7 inch) cake tin.

§   Sift the flour, salt and spices in a large mixing bowl, making sure you aerate the flour well.

§   In a separate bowl, whisk the sugar and butter together until pale-looking. Now add your beaten eggs to that mixture slowly, one at a time, and keep whisking so as not to curdle.

§   Now gently fold in the mixed spiced flour. Take your time and don't knock out the air from the flour. Finally, add the brandy-soaked fruits, nuts, peel, zest and treacle. Keep folding (do not beat).

§   Now transfer the batter to the cake tin and place in the oven to bake. Do not feel the need to check on this cake for the first 4 hours – it takes a long time but is well worth the wait.

§   When cooked (a skewer inserted into the centre should come out cleanly), leave the cake in the tin for a good 30–40 minutes before turning out onto a wired rack. When cold, turn it over and make a few little holes evenly over the base with a skewer and drip more alcohol into your cake. Repeat at intervals as Christmas nears, always carefully rewrapping the cake in baking paper and keeping it airtight afterwards.

§   Now you can ice and dress your cake, either with fondant icing or Royal icing, but start with a base layer of marzipan (see page 28).

MARZIPAN

PREPARATION TIME 10 mins

INGREDIENTS

250g (9oz) ground almonds
130g (4½oz) icing sugar
130g (4½oz) caster sugar
1 egg yolk (20g)

METHOD

§   Combine all the dry ingredients, then add the egg yolk and stir in until the mixture is smooth.

§   Form the mixture into a ball and wrap in cling film until needed.

§   When ready to decorate the cake, roll out to a thickness of 5mm (¼ inch) and lay over the cake before covering with your choice of royal or fondant icing.

ROYAL ICING

PREPARATION TIME 20 mins

INGREDIENTS

700g (1½lb) icing sugar
3 egg whites (120g)
1 tsp liquid glycerine
2 tsp lemon juice

METHOD

§   Sift the icing sugar into a bowl. In a separate bowl, whisk the egg whites until frothy. Now add the icing sugar, folding it in a little bit at a time. Add the glycerine and lemon juice and beat until stiff.

§   Now cover the cake with the icing, swirling it into soft peaks.

FONDANT ICING

PREPARATION TIME 20 mins

INGREDIENTS

500g (1lb 2oz) icing sugar,
   plus extra for dusting
1 large egg white (45g)
Few drops of vanilla extract
40g (1½oz) liquid glucose
   (about 2 tbsp)
Cornflour, for dusting

METHOD

§   Sift the icing sugar into a bowl. Add the egg white, vanilla and glucose and stir. This will become very stiff, so work it with your hands to soften.

§   When it is all mixed, roll it into a ball and on a worktop dusted with cornflour and icing sugar you can roll it out to cover the cake as desired.

RED CABBAGE SAUERKRAUT

Fermented foods have been important to many civilisations as they keep for two or more months, through periods when fresh food was scarce. In the past we did not just feast, we also had to conserve food to survive poor harvests or deep winters. Sauerkraut may have a modern German name but the recipe is steeped in time – as well as in salt. It was probably brought to Europe from China. If you find it a little too tart, simply rinse under some cold water before you heat or eat it.

Often made with white cabbage, this crunchy, dark-red sauerkraut is one of my favourites. Apart from the wonderful burst of colour it brings to a meal, it is a great foil for meats or plain food. You can serve it warmed or cold, with any meal or as a salad. What's more, it's packed with fibre as well as healthy minerals, enzymes and phytonutrients.

PREPARATION TIME 15 mins, plus fermenting

INGREDIENTS

1 small red cabbage,
   core and outer leaves
   removed, finely shredded
2 medium onions,
   finely shredded
4 tsp Maldon sea salt
1 tsp mustard seeds
1 tsp coriander seeds,
   toasted
½–1 tsp chilli flakes

METHOD

§   In a large bowl, combine the cabbage and onions, then massage in the salt, seeds and chilli flakes. Leave to sweat for 1–2 hours. A natural fluid will collect at the bottom of the bowl – keep this for later.

§   When ready, transfer the vegetables to a sterilised, airtight jar (see page 308). Really pack them in, then pour over the reserved liquid to cover the veg by about an inch. (If there is not enough fluid, more brine can be made with a ratio of 1 teaspoon of salt to 200ml/7fl oz water.)

§   Place a sterilised stone, ceramic or glass object into the jar to keep the veg submerged as much as possible. Place the jar out of direct sunlight for 3–10 days, depending on how much you like the flavours to develop. You can store the sauerkraut in the sealed jar in the fridge for up to 6 months.

SPICED BEETROOT CHUTNEY

Chutneys originated from the Indian subcontinent, and just like pickles they were an excellent way of preserving vegetables and fruit. Today there is not the same practical necessity for preserves, but they remain a delicious accompaniment to cheese or alongside roast meats and stews.

Just as pickling vinegar is used to preserve fruit or vegetables, in the case of a chutney, sugar and spices are added as well and the vegetables tend to be cooked for longer.

PREPARATION TIME 10 mins   COOKING TIME 1 hr, plus cooling

INGREDIENTS

1·5kg (3¼lb) raw beetroot, trimmed, peeled and diced (wear gloves!)

3 onions, chopped

3 eating apples, peeled and grated

Zest and juice of 3 oranges

2 tbsp white or yellow mustard seeds

1 tbsp coriander seeds

1 tbsp ground cloves

1 tbsp ground cinnamon

700ml (1¼ pints) red wine vinegar

700g (1½lb) golden granulated sugar

METHOD

§   In a large saucepan, mix together all the ingredients, then bring to a gentle simmer and cook for an hour, stirring occasionally, until the chutney is thick and the beetroot is fork-tender.

§   While the chutney is cooking, clean and sterilise the jars (see page 308).

§   Pull the pan off the heat and let the chutney sit for 10 minutes, then carefully spoon it into the jars and seal whilst hot.

§   You can eat this straight away but it will be even better after a month. This will keep for up to 6 months in a cool dark place. Once opened, refrigerate and eat within 2 months.

CHAPTER THREE

ADVENT

❋ STRICTLY SPEAKING, ❋ IN CHRISTIAN TERMS, THE PROCESS OF PREPARING FOR CHRISTMAS BEGINS WITH ADVENT.

There are forty days of Advent, which begins on 11 November with the Feast of St Martin of Tours, although for the great majority of traditions in Western Europe, Advent nowadays commences on the fourth Sunday before Christmas – the Sunday nearest to St Andrew's Day (30 November).

THE PRESENT FOUR-WEEK ADVENT WAS INTRODUCED in the eleventh century, and the devout were supposed to fast during this period – or at least on three out of the seven days of the week. It always sounds to me a little like the 5/2 diet that is so popular today!

The beginning of Advent sets the date for our next Highclere meeting, at which we ensure we are on track with our events – from Christmas workshops to carols and fairs, dinners, receptions, readings or creating a Santa Claus Grotto.

WORKSHOPS &
WREATH MAKING

FATHER CHRISTMAS HAS WORKSHOPS AND SO DOES Highclere, although ours tend to focus on wreaths and decorations rather than making gifts for friends and family. Looking at photographs of beautiful wreaths and admiring the artistry with which I cannot hope to compete, I pick up the phone to Henrietta (wife of Castle Manager John Gundill and florist extraordinaire) to ask her if she will come and lead some workshops here at the Castle. From plain circles of holly or mistletoe to hoops decorated with dried orange, cinnamon, pine cones, ribbons and tartan, a door wreath immediately says 'Welcome!'. At Highclere, Christmas for our guests and visitors really starts with our tall walnut front doors, studded with black ironmongery, oiled and weathered, and festively decorated with two matching wreaths.

The circular shape of the wreath, with no beginning or end, is supposed to represent eternity, or life never-ending, whilst the use of evergreens represents eternal life. Johann Hinrich Wichern (1808–81), a Lutheran clergyman in Hamburg, is known to have made a wreath with the thought of involving children in Bible study. This wreath, however, was one that was adorned with Advent candles and designed to hang horizontally. Others later took up and adapted the idea to create the wreaths that we have today, hung on doors or set on tables as centrepieces. However, the tradition of hanging a wreath on your door precedes the Christian celebration of Christmas; Romans made them to celebrate the winter festival of Saturnalia, and the custom may even extend further back than that.

These days, wreaths are traditionally hung on the first Sunday of Advent, or perhaps a little later. Accordingly, our workshop days are scattered throughout the end of November. Thus Christmas begins to take shape with a little work, a lot of goodwill, some tea or prosecco (depending on the time of day), spiced orange scones or slices of fruit cake.

Reward yourself and your friends after wreath making with some
SPICED ORANGE
SCONES
PAGE 54

TO MAKE A WREATH YOURSELF YOU WILL NEED either a pre-bought wreath base (diameter 45–50cm/18–20 inches), or a few 90cm/3ft lengths of dogwood or willow; florist or fine garden wire; secateurs; and your choice of other foliage, berries, flowers and/ or ribbons in your colour scheme. For example, greenery such as spruce and holly, offset with bronze chrysanthemums, dried oranges, cinnamon stick bundles, pine cones and deep red and gold ribbon. Or explore your flowerbeds for hydrangea flowers, umbels, rosemary, bay leaves, viburnum, holly or Christmas box.

If you are making the wreath base yourself, wind the shoots around your knee or foot to create a circle and tuck in the ends of the shoots or fix them in place with a short length of wire. Carry on with more shoots until you have the thickness that you require.

Think of the wreath as four quadrants. You want some elements of symmetry but not too much. Wire small bundles of foliage together, each with a brighter decoration, then attach the bundles to the wreath base with more wire. Work from the six o'clock position, making your way up each side, spacing them evenly. Keep back some of the bigger flowers and other decorations to create a focal point either at the bottom or to the lower right quadrant, tying these in last for a final flourish.

STIR-UP SUNDAY

'STIR-UP SUNDAY' IS THE LAST SUNDAY BEFORE ADVENT, which, in four years out of seven, is the next-to-last Sunday in November and traditionally the day when the Christmas pudding is made. The collect for that Sunday in church suggests:

Stir up, we beseech thee, O Lord, the wills of thy faithful people; that they, plenteously bringing forth the fruit of good works, may by thee be plenteously rewarded; through Jesus Christ our Lord. Amen.

From a practical point of view the best chefs and cooks plan and prepare ahead, and you can make a Christmas pudding months in advance because the high alcohol content stops the mixture spoiling. Making Christmas puddings has always been a family event; it is so crammed full of ingredients that it is hard work to stir, making it an ideal job for many willing hands together.

Christmas pudding, or plum pudding, really became an essential part of Christmas Day during Victorian times. Charles Dickens describes the scene in *A Christmas Carol*:

Mrs Cratchit left the room alone – too nervous to bear witnesses – to take the pudding up and bring it in... Hallo! A great deal of steam!

Our favourite recipe for
**CHRISTMAS
PUDDING**
PAGE 57

*The pudding was out of the copper which smells like a washing-day.
That was the cloth. A smell like an eating-house and a pastrycook's
next door to each other, with a laundress's next door to that. That
was the pudding. In half a minute Mrs Cratchit entered – flushed, but
smiling proudly – with the pudding, like a speckled cannon-ball, so
hard and firm, blazing in half of half-a-quarter of ignited brandy, and
bedight with Christmas holly stuck into the top.*

There are many different versions of Christmas pudding, possibly
because it was often a recipe handed down through families by example
and experience, rather than written down. Generally, there are supposed
to be thirteen ingredients, to represent Christ and the Twelve Apostles.
My recipe, which comes from a lovely lady called Queenie who worked
for my mother, has sixteen different ingredients, but if you added the
three Magi to Christ and the Twelve Apostles, you would arrive at sixteen,
so I believe it is still valid!

ADVENT CALENDARS

POSSIBLY THE MOST WELL-KNOWN ASPECT OF ADVENT
these days is the Advent calendar. Of course, the whole concept of
Christmas is grounded in memories and an Advent calendar is a physical
reminder of the excitement of the gradual build-up to Christmas Day
itself. The ones we had as children just had a saying or a picture each time
you opened a door, but now they often contain small gifts or chocolates
instead. Whichever one you choose, they are a lovely way to count off
the days until Santa Claus arrives: a magical treat for children of all
ages – even grown-up ones!

Originally, Advent calendars were hand-drawn on walls or in books
by families, but the formal idea of a picture with doors that can be torn
off or opened began in Germany in the 1850s. Thomas Mann's novel
Buddenbrooks, which follows four generations of a wealthy German family,
memorably describes a homemade Advent calendar that Nanny Ida had
made for her charge, little Hanno J, who was so excited as he opened
the final little door to see the Christmas tree.

From these handmade versions, commercially manufactured ones soon
followed, but it was not until the 1950s that these calendars were filled
with little chocolate or other tiny gifts. The market today is awash with
different designs – from traditional children's versions of the nativity scene
to luxury offerings for grown-up children from major perfume houses.
Irrespective of your choice, I hope that they are now all ready hanging on
the wall, waiting for 1 December.

And, since it *is* nearly December, it's time for a winter's tale...

ONCE UPON A TIME IN 800 AD
CHRIST'S MAESSE AT HIGHCLERE

THE TRAVELLER PULLED HIS HEAVY, DAMP CLOAK
around him, anxiously scanning the clouds looming over the bare hilltop.
Largely visible from all around, the high silhouette of the hill with broken
walls at its summit marked his route: the more distant, steeper side led
to the wooded entrance of the track which wound through the trees to
Highclere. His horse shook his head sideways, trying to avoid the sleet.
They were both tired, having left Winchester early that morning and,
although he was sure it could not be much further, every mile seemed to
take longer in the short winter day.

To his right the ground fell away sharply and the traveller peered
cautiously ahead at the dense mass of innumerable trees. The slender grey

stems of the birch trees stepped before him, bending barely in the wintry squall. He knew that they should ward off any evil spirits and give him courage, and they did indeed seem to reflect what little light there was.

As the trail became ever more indistinct, it seemed far less familiar than it had been in the summer. Tense with concentration, he gave a last encouragement to his horse to pick up the pace. Finally, they turned up an incline and, relieved, he saw a faint glow up ahead. The horse picked his way through a palisade and into the courtyard. Gratefully, the traveller dismounted, stretched and patted the dark damp neck; his horse's breath was steaming in the air and he shook himself, whickering. The thatched stables were at the back of the collection of timber-framed buildings and would offer them both somewhere to eat and sleep: a refuge from the relentless wet and dark weather.

His plan was to stay at least until Epiphany on the sixth day of January in order to inspect Bishop Cyneberht's demesne and accounts at Highclere, and to review those at Ecchinswell and Overton, before returning eventually to Winchester. As Bishop of Winchester, Cyneberht was one of the wealthiest men in England and the accounts had to be gathered together annually, before the official year end on Lady Day (25 March).

The traveller led his horse into a stall and rubbed him down, piling up hay and propping up the saddle to dry. Walking across the muddied stones, past the faint shapes of the oven houses and water wells, he pushed open a heavy door and stepped into the hall to at last shake off his cloak, stamping his boots to rid the worst of the snow. The enormous fire across the room was piled high with thick logs, whilst candles gave light to tables decorated with flagons and meats, although the edges of the hall remained indistinct.

Another ten or twelve people were gathered there. A tall young man kicked a huge log further into the fire whilst a man in a fur-lined jerkin looked up from the table and smiled. 'Welcome! You are in good time for Christes Maesse.'

The traveller approached the fire, glad to stand in its warming glow. The dancing flames crackled and flitted, creating warmth and comradeship, making it a place for stories and songs whilst the candles guttered and smoked, the tallow giving out an unpleasant aroma. Although Highclere owned bee hives which lined the 'hunig weg', a track that ran along the top of the downs, proper wax candles were expensive, luxury items which had to be accounted for and so were kept for special occasions or sent to Winchester.

The traveller gratefully accepted a cup of mead and exchanged news of what was happening at Winchester. There had been rumours of huge wooden ships with dragons at the prow seen off the south coast and they had all heard what had happened at Lindisfarne. The traveller knew of no more reports so perhaps the invaders would go somewhere else, they mulled. They could only hope and pray.

Soothing and sustaining
for centuries:
PORRIDGE
PAGE 48

THE STATUE ᴏꜰ CHARLEMAGNE

IN 800 AD, KING CHARLEMAGNE, KNOWN AS THE FATHER of Europe, travelled to Rome where, on 1 December, he held a council that would change the shape of Europe.

Conqueror of the Saxons, patron of the Holy Roman Church, robust and tall in frame, a great hunter and ruler, he knelt in the church of St Peter on 25 December to be anointed Holy Roman Emperor, in the name of the Father, Son and Holy Ghost, just as if he were heralding in a new epoch.

A monumental head of this ancient king sits at Highclere in the lee of the Yew Trees, just near the Secret Garden, because my husband's family claims to be descended from him. Extraordinarily, Highclere was itself already in existence at this time, albeit in a slightly different format to today. Owned and administered by the Bishop of Winchester for fifty years by this point, it was a collection of buildings and an early chapel in which to pray, whilst the surrounding farmland and grazing provided a living for some ten families.

THE BLEAK MIDWINTER
BECOMES A TIME FOR FESTIVITY

THE VENERABLE BEDE (672–735 AD) NOTED 'THAT THE ancient people of the Angli began the year on the 25 December when we now celebrate the birthday of our Lord'.

Later, as the Vikings settled in to England, they did not quite embrace Christianity, but they did not forbid it, and so there was peace, at least for the moment. In another eighty years, though, Alfred the Great, King of Wessex (849–899 AD), would defend his country against the Vikings. Establishing his capital at Winchester, he would enshrine Christmas Day and the twelve succeeding days until Epiphany as a holiday, the precursor of today's bank holidays. Alfred nobly summed up his ambitions:

I desired to live worthily as long as I lived, and to leave after my life, to the men who should come after me, the memory of me in good works.

Winter celebrations were, without doubt, a highlight of the often bleak, dark days of the season, and an encouragement to look ahead towards the better weather and longer days of spring. Since the short days meant it was not possible to spend much time out of doors, less agricultural work could be completed in the winter months.

Highclere's hall would have been decorated with what the women could find in the land around the house at that time of year. Holly and mistletoe

If Jack Frost is nipping at your nose, and you have a hand free, Christmas is the time for
ROASTED
CHESTNUTS
PAGE 50

would have grown abundantly in the woods around the manor, along with blackthorn and crab apples.

Thus, from early times, Christes Maesse became a popular party season, when people would celebrate and take stock. More than a thousand years after our traveller arrived at Highclere, Christina Rossetti beautifully captured the wintry conditions in her poem 'In the bleak midwinter':

In the bleak mid-winter, frosty wind made moan,
Earth stood hard as iron, water like a stone;
Snow had fallen, snow on snow, snow on snow,
In the bleak mid-winter, long ago.

G E O G R A P H Y

1/ The Saloon is decorated with leather wall coverings, but where are they from?

2/ Where did Isobel and Matthew Crawley live before they arrived at Downton Abbey?

3/ Following her marriage, Lady Edith becomes a Marchioness, but of where?

4/ Where does the Dowager Countess of Grantham live?

5/ In Anglo-Saxon times, Highclere was owned by the Bishops of Winchester, but which Kingdom did it fall within?

6/ Where do Lady Rose and Atticus Aldridge spend their honeymoon?

7/ Where is Lady Rose MacClare's family home, and where is it in reality?

8/ Henry Talbot and Charlie Rogers both take part in a sports car race, in which Charlie later crashes and dies. Where is the race held?

9/ Mercia bedroom at Highclere is named after one of the Anglo-Saxon Kingdoms, but can you name the remaining three?

10/ The Napoleon armchair sits in the Music Room at Highclere, but where did Napoleon die in exile?

11/ Highclere Castle is in which English county?

12/ Queen Caroline's bedroom was named in her honour when she came to stay at Highclere, but where was she from?

W H O   S A I D . . .

13/ 'What is a weekend?'   14/ 'Sympathy butters no parsnips'

15/ The Duke of Wellington visited Highclere in July 1831 and famously responded to the threat of revelations about his private life with; 'Publish and be' ... what?

H I G H C L E R E   T O D A Y

16/ How old is the oldest member of staff at Highclere?

17/ What are the names of the pigs kept at Highclere?

ANSWERS

1/ Spain 2/ Manchester 3/ Hexham 4/ The Dower House in Downton Abbey village 5/ Wessex
6/ Venice, Italy 7/ Duneagle Castle, Scotland; Inverary Castle, Argyll, Scotland 8/ Brooklands race track
9/ East Anglia, Wessex and Northumbria 10/ Longwood House, St Helena 11/ Hampshire 12/ Ansbach,
Brandenburg-Ansbach, Germany 13/ The Dowager Countess 14/ Mrs Patmore 15/ 'Publish and be damned.'
16/ 94 17/ Thelma and Louise

47

PORRIDGE

A bowl of porridge is unbeatable at the start of the day on a winter's morning.

Here is the basic way to cook the ubiquitous winter favourite, however, often I will add a tablespoon of oatmeal, linseed or chia seeds. Sometimes I might add some blueberries or a teaspoon of honeycomb, it depends on my mood and the morning. I like using the big flakes of oats and sometimes add almond milk (unsweetened, nothing added) as well as water to cook it.

Eat it how you will and enjoy it. As a health benefit it is high in fibre and minerals and helps lower cholesterol – just don't add sugar, please.

PREPARATION TIME 2 mins   COOKING TIME 5–10 mins   SERVES 4–6

INGREDIENTS

200g (7oz) porridge oats
1·4 litres (2½ pints) water
Pinch of salt, to taste

METHOD

§   Put the oats into a large saucepan, pour in the water and add the salt. Some people worry about adding salt, but it deepens the flavour of the oats.

§   Gently heat, stirring continuously to avoid sticking or burning the pan for 5–10 minutes.

§   Remove from the heat when the oats have absorbed the water and/or reached the desired consistency.

ROASTED CHESTNUTS

Think of laid-back Christmas songs and you can hear Nat King Cole singing:

Chestnuts roasting on an open fire
Jack Frost nipping at your nose
Yule-tide carols being sung by a choir
And folks dressed up like Eskimos.

The recipe below is for cooking chestnuts in an oven, but we also put them on a shovel and cook them in a fire, then tip them onto a plate, allow to cool, peel and dip each one into a little salt – just delicious.

If you pass the church and come in through Highclere Park gates by Clerewood Lodge you might notice an old tall chestnut tree. The soil here is slightly acidic and this is in fact an eating chestnut rather than a decorative 'horse chestnut' tree. Starchy chestnuts have been eaten for thousands of years, although this tree has only been here for a few hundred. Before wheat or potatoes, the chestnut was a main source of carbohydrate during the winter throughout Europe, and it was traditional to eat roasted chestnuts in Portugal at the start of Advent (St Martin's Day). Apart from roasting, they can be puréed, canned or conserved as marrons glacé.

PREPARATION TIME **10 mins**   COOKING TIME **30 mins**

INGREDIENTS

320g (11oz) chestnuts
  (bigger and shinier ones
  are best)

METHOD

§   Preheat the oven to 200°C/400°F/Gas mark 6.

§   Laying each on its flat side, carefully cut a long slit into each chestnut. Place into a roasting tray, one layer deep and not too overcrowded.

§   Roast for up to 30 minutes or until the skins split open further.

§   Allow to cool, then peel away the shells and remove the inner brown membrane, then they are ready to eat.

ROASTED FIGS

Figs, like so many other delicious things, were brought to Britain by the Romans. They are one of the world's oldest trees, featuring in early historical documents including the Bible. Figs have been grown against the south-facing garden walls of the Castle for centuries and you can serve them as pudding with Greek yoghurt, toss them into a salad with some toasted nuts or enjoy them with some Italian prosciutto.

PREPARATION TIME less than 5 mins   COOKING TIME 8 mins   SERVES 2–4

INGREDIENTS

8 ripe figs

A drizzle of runny honey

Salt and pepper

METHOD

§   Preheat the oven to 180°C/350°F/Gas mark 4.

§   Score the figs from top to bottom four times. Place on baking paper on a baking tray with a drizzle of honey and season to taste. Place in the oven for just 6–8 minutes.

§   Remove and serve.

SPICED ORANGE SCONES

PREPARATION TIME **10 mins**   COOKING TIME **20 mins**   MAKES **8 medium scones**

INGREDIENTS

225g (8oz) self-raising flour,
   plus extra for dusting
½ tsp salt
1 tsp ground cardamom
Zest of 1 orange
60g (2½oz) unsalted butter,
   cold and cut into cubes
40g (1½oz) caster sugar
140–150ml (4½–5fl oz)
   milk
Beaten egg, to glaze
   (optional)

METHOD

§   Preheat the oven to 200°C/400°F/Gas mark 6.

§   Put the flour, salt, cardamom, orange zest and butter in a large bowl. Using your fingers, lightly rub the ingredients together until it resembles breadcrumbs.

§   Mix in the sugar and make a well in the centre. Add the milk, little by little, and mix with a fork until the dough just comes together.

§   Knead the dough for a minute or so until it is soft and spongy. Don't over-knead as this will make the scones tough. Add a little extra milk if the dough is too dry.

§   Place the dough on a floured surface and roll out to 2cm (¾ inch) thickness.

§   Use a 6cm (2½ inch) pastry cutter to cut out the scones. If desired, brush the scones with beaten egg to make them glossy.

§   Place the scones on a lightly floured baking sheet and place in the oven for 17–20 minutes, until the scones have risen and are golden. Best served warm.

FRUIT BISCUITS

Something of a curiosity, this recipe dates from about 1810/11 and was found in the papers of the 2nd Countess of Carnarvon. We have tried these and found them interesting, but perhaps not worth a solid hour's whisking!

Infuse any kind of fruit in an earthenware jar placed in a kettle of water til they are all of mash.

Rub the fruit thro a sieve... a pound of sugar sifted to a pound of the pulp.

Beat them together with a strong whisk for an hour with the white of an egg to each pound of fruit.

Put them into paper or drop them on paper and dry them in a stove or warm place.

CHRISTMAS PUDDING

PREPARATION TIME **30 mins**   COOKING TIME **15 mins**   SERVES **8**

INGREDIENTS

400g (14oz) mixed
    dried fruit
150g (5oz) sultanas
100g (3½oz) currants
40g (1½oz) dried figs,
    roughly chopped
30g (1¼oz) glacé cherries
10g (¼oz) crystallised
    ginger
40g (1½oz) candied peel
125ml (4½fl oz) Madeira
75g (3oz) self-raising flour
150g (5oz) soft light brown
    sugar
½ tsp mixed spice
Pinch of salt
Finely grated zest of
    1 unwaxed lemon and
    1 unwaxed orange
50g (2oz) blanched
    almonds, chopped
30g (1¼oz) grated carrots
75g (3oz) fresh
    breadcrumbs
150g (5oz) suet
1 egg, beaten
1 tbsp golden syrup
125ml (4fl oz) rum
125ml (4fl oz) stout
75ml (3fl oz) milk
4–5 pound coins
    wrapped in silver foil
    (not when making
    months in advance)

METHOD

§   Pile all the dried fruit and peel into a mixing bowl. Pour over the Madeira and cover with cling film. Leave to soak overnight.

§   The next morning, mix together the flour, light brown sugar, spice, salt, zests, almonds, carrot and breadcrumbs in a large mixing bowl.

§   Gradually stir in the softer ingredients – the suet, the beaten egg and golden syrup – then pour in the rum, stout and milk.

§   Rope in as many people as possible to stir everything up. Everyone should turn the wooden spoon around in a clockwise direction, from east to west, making a wish as they do so.

§   Finally, add the soaked fruit and keep stirring. Taste it and add what you feel it needs.

§   Carefully grease a 1·5kg (2½-pint) pudding basin, and spoon the mixture in so it is about three-quarters full. Push in the wrapped pound coins, if using. Cut a round of greaseproof paper to fit the top, then cover and wrap the pudding bowl in foil to ensure it is watertight.

§   Steam for 4 hours, checking the water level regularly. Always top up with hot water so as not to interrupt the cooking time – this will also save you getting a soggy pudding.

§   Take the pan off the heat. Check the pudding is cooked by inserting a skewer through the foil and paper. If it comes out clean, it is done; if not, return to the heat.

§   Allow to cool and store in a pantry or cool place until Christmas Day.

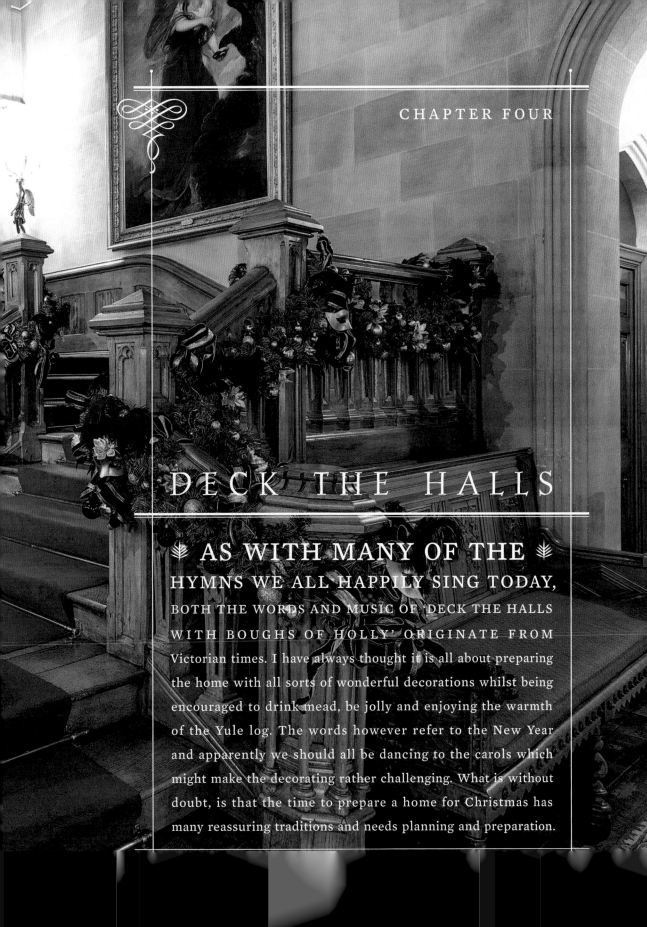

CHAPTER FOUR

DECK THE HALLS

❧ AS WITH MANY OF THE ❧ HYMNS WE ALL HAPPILY SING TODAY, BOTH THE WORDS AND MUSIC OF 'DECK THE HALLS WITH BOUGHS OF HOLLY' ORIGINATE FROM

Victorian times. I have always thought it is all about preparing the home with all sorts of wonderful decorations whilst being encouraged to drink mead, be jolly and enjoying the warmth of the Yule log. The words however refer to the New Year and apparently we should all be dancing to the carols which might make the decorating rather challenging. What is without doubt, is that the time to prepare a home for Christmas has many reassuring traditions and needs planning and preparation.

GIVEN THE NUMBER OF ROOMS IN THE CASTLE, WE HAVE to make practical choices about which we are going to decorate. It is also better to have a theme, so that it all hangs together.

The Saloon at Highclere is the heart of the house and its sheer size dictates that it is the location for the main tree, whilst a smaller one goes in the Library. Candles are scattered throughout the Castle and garlands are wound around mantelpieces, the dining table is set, clusters of poinsettias are positioned on the tables in the Gallery and holly is trimmed and put in rows of vases. As the Christmas cards arrive they are set on the grand piano, on tables, or – my mother's choice – hung on lengths of ribbon and strung up around the bookshelves.

NATURE INSPIRES

2 DECEMBER. THE BARE BROWN BRANCHES OF TREES, the muted colours of distant fields and the short days remind me that December is considered by many to be the start of winter. It is certainly starting to feel like it. Walking down towards the gardens, the cold air tingling on my face and the last of the scattered leaves scuffing under my feet, it is a quiet, lonely time of year.

Happily wrapped inside a scarf and coat, a bevy of dogs running around, I have a practical project in mind: I am hoping to find some foliage and berries to provide texture and colour to help us decorate the Castle, both inside and out, for our Christmas public opening. I look out for the bursts of colour – winter berries, spindle plants, euonymus and hollies, both variegated and plain. Field hedgerows also have different textures, some of

PREVIOUS PAGES
The Oak Staircase which leads
from the Saloon at the heart of
the Castle

which can be gathered and brought inside. Highclere's winter garden holds its own magic, rich with rosehips sprinkled with frost, tiny ice sculptures suspended from uneven stems and cobwebs silhouetted with dewy delicacy.

There is never a day when I don't feel lucky to be out walking with the dogs in such a beautiful landscape. The dogs are impervious to the weather, snuffling through thickets of grass, happily exploring all the hollows around the knuckled roots of the beech trees, looking for small puddles of water to drink. It must taste especially good. The dense shapes of the splendid cedar trees cut horizontally across bare vistas, the aged beech timbers seem to be nearly grey, with the sharper white birch catching the light in the woodland.

Nature lies modestly dormant yet remains starkly beautiful. I am not the only admirer, though. The birds remain in residence and will only survive these months with the help of winter berries, acorns and seeds scavenged from the frost-silvered fields. Well aware that I am in competition with them as I head out with the secateurs, I try to ensure we bolster the birds' meagre winter pickings with fat balls and seed tables.

I hear the robin before I see him. Just inside the wooden gate, the little bright scarlet bird is perched on a bare branch. He is singing passionately, probably to ward off other robins: this is his corner of the garden. The Anglo-Saxons called this little bird a ruddock (meaning redbreast), then eight hundred years later the Tudors added 'robin' to the name and, with

ABOVE
One of the Cedars of Lebanon
in Highclere Park

61

their splash of colour, considered them lucky. These charming little birds still appear on the Christmas cards that decorate the Saloon and cover the piano in the Drawing Room.

I spy some holly growing under gnarled oak trees. Birds are able to eat the berries in small quantities but they are poisonous for humans, making them unsuitable for table decorations. I decide to move on. A group of native, green-and-white-tinted hellebores nestle under a yew tree, where they are slowly spreading a pool of winter cheer. Happily, I have seen some large shrubs of evergreen winter box, cornus, viburnum, dogwood and unpruned hydrangea heads along with pine cones and stems of long grasses. As children we would spray long broken twigs gold and silver, making a terrible mess in the process. Nevertheless, they can look rather good and be used to hang baubles on, whilst moss will disguise the trappings needed to hold such arrangements upright. Anything I find that is wet from the weather can be stored in the Beaters' Room or the old garages to dry until needed.

A little later, once more trailing a procession of dogs, I return to the Georgian courtyard via the broad gravel drive which winds around behind the Castle, where a group of spindly yew trees with ivy scrambling up their trunks reach towards the winter skies. I am always in two minds about ivy as it is reputed to be a harbinger of doom and, I believe, compromises the health of the trees. Yet this ivy has probably been here for a hundred years at least, far longer than I. It covers the remains of the old church that lay tucked up to the west side of the house. Two thousand years ago, Romans wore crowns and wreaths made of ivy; Pliny tells of how he carefully trailed it up trellis in his garden and considered it to be the winter vine. It flowers and fruits long after anything else, and thus bees will be found humming around it even quite late in the year. More prosaically, it looks fabulous with yew sprigs to create the dark foil of background colour for our arrangements on mantelpieces and staircases.

From here it is round to the west side of the Castle, where globes of mistletoe hang in profusion. It is usually, tantalisingly, just out of reach, but I have found that if I clamber onto the bonnet of a high 4×4 car I can, in fact, reach some of it. My son, worried for my wellbeing, kindly asks me to ensure someone is with me on such a foray. My husband asks after the condition of the car bonnet. Mistletoe became a symbol of reconciliation and love from Norse mythology – something my husband might like to take note of!

In fact, mistletoe is steeped in myth as both sacred and medicinal. The tradition of kissing under the mistletoe originated in Ancient Greece, then became part of the Roman festival of Saturnalia and thus, with its associations with fertility, was incorporated into marriage ceremonies, too. Whilst the Druids traditionally cut mistletoe from oak trees, I find it grows best here high amongst the lime trees (it likes the light and thus is not found in woodland) but I have also managed to propagate it by squeezing the white currant-like berries into small scratches I made in the bark of some of the apple trees, where it has taken well and is much lower and easier to pick.

With the dogs emerging from forays in hedgerows and the obligatory rootle around the greenhouses, their coats steaming into the cool winter air, my reconnaissance is complete. Ideas and plans metamorphosing, I retreat indoors to warm up with some steaming hot coffee.

RIGHT
Mistletoe drying in the front hall ready for use in decorations

THE FLOWER ROOM, SITUATED IN THE BASEMENT NEXT to the Egyptian Exhibition, is the nerve centre for decorating the marquees that will house the Christmas Fair and serve festive afternoon teas. Ever practical, the Castle's Victorian builders supplied it with its own staircase and door to the outside, shared with the original coal cellars. Head Gardener Paul Barker and his team gather huge piles of budded ivy and various evergreens and leave them at the top of the flower-room steps. Secateurs and gloves at the ready, I start by filling some forty-five terracotta pots with floral foam, before dragging in the greenery and cutting it into suitable lengths. Baubles wired in amongst the greenery add a splash of colour, and with a ribbon tied round the outside they are ready for the banqueting team to deploy round the various tearooms.

As far as the outside of the Castle is concerned, we rely heavily on a profusion of Christmas trees, carefully placed for maximum impact. In the courtyard at the back of the Castle the gardeners have wedged one nine-foot and four seven-foot trees into sturdy containers weighed down with a heavy mixture of soil and sand. On the opposite side of the building, two more nine-foot trees go on either side of the front door whilst a total of twenty-four five-foot equally spaced trees line the driveway.

The first job once the trees are in position is to wind around the strings of lights. I have found a novel way to complete this in record time by initiating a game-show-style competition (sadly without the witty commentary of a professional commentator) adjudicated by Sally and her chief decorator, Sarah. The hastily recruited competitors launch themselves at their respective trees and – voilà – twenty-seven trees are lit, to Sarah's mildly disdainful yet laughing approval. Next the baubles have to go on, each carefully and firmly wired onto the trees to withstand the often gusty winds that blow through this part of the world. It is a labour of love in the cold, with scratched and sore hands to administer to afterwards, but the finished effect is well worth the effort.

DRESSING For DINNER

HIGHCLERE'S DINING ROOM, HUNG IN YELLOW SILKS with huge, important portraits, is very much a statement in itself, and so exactly how to decorate it for Christmas gives rise to much careful thought. In some ways, the challenge is highly appropriate, given that King Charles I, whose magnificent portrait by Anthony van Dyck dominates the room, directed his noblemen and gentry to return to their landed estates to keep up the tradition of Christmas generosity in bleak midwinters.

However, in 1641 the King led his country into civil war and, following his capture and eventual execution by Cromwell's forces, the victorious Puritans banned Christmas, deeming it a Catholic celebration replete with sinful

merrymaking. Pro-Christmas rioting broke out in several cities in England, Canterbury in particular. For weeks the city was controlled by rioters who defiantly decorated doorways with holly and ivy, shouted Royalist slogans and sang carols – which were then transformed into songs of protest – danced, feasted, roasted apples on fires and played cards.

Christmas festivities were legally reinstated by King Charles II when he regained the throne in 1660 and were probably even noisier and more raucous than they had been in his father's day. In 1683, Charles commissioned Sir Christopher Wren to build a royal palace at Winchester modelled after the Palace of Versailles, though on a somewhat smaller scale, with sweeping views, walks and gardens which would descend to the city's cathedral. Just before this time, Geordie's ancestor, courtier to Charles II, bought Highclere House and Estate, which had been in private ownership since the Bishops of Winchester lost it in the 1550s, to ensure he was close to the King's new palace but, equally, not too close.

It was not until the mid-nineteenth century that celebrating Christmas became really fashionable and accepted once again. Christmas Day had long been considered a holiday but in 1834 the Bank of England reduced the number of holidays from thirty-three to four, of which Christmas Day remained one. In some ways the name was only formalised with the Bank Holidays Act 1871, which then also included Boxing Day. It was during this period that Highclere House was transformed into the

ABOVE
A festive garland decorates
the fireplace in the
State Dining Room

Italianate-inspired castle in which we celebrate today what is largely a Victorian-inspired Christmas.

This early on in December, I settle on the mantelpiece as the best space in the Dining Room to decorate. Along its length we create an evergreen decoration which will last a month, and which is set with cream pillar candles or bowls of artificial flowers and a garland of trailing ivy and pine cones. The table and sideboard will be decorated with fresh flowers and foliage, so these must wait until just before Christmas or they will wilt.

PAPERWHITES & POINSETTIAS

CHRISTMAS DECORATIONS CONJURE UP MEMORIES OF scents such as pine and cinnamon, cloves, hot chocolate, gingerbread, oranges and spiced apples. However, the other fragrances that the gardeners endeavour to encourage are those from hyacinths and paperwhite narcissi.

My husband peruses various bulb catalogues and carefully chooses some new hyacinths as well as the ones that he remembers his father liked. Paul will then plant these in terracotta pots with just the tip showing above the soil and leave them in a cold dark shed for 8–10 weeks. The flower spikes will gradually push up, at which point Paul will bring them out and into the orangery, which is cool but light. He then lines up the various plants and colours in rows, watching them anxiously each morning and trying to encourage their even growth, as they look best grouped in threes or fives in large planters in the Castle. They also make excellent Christmas presents.

Heating is always in short supply in the Castle, which is best for both hyacinths and the paperwhites. At least the heating is better now than in the

RIGHT
Poinsettias and holly bring the
outside inside at Christmas

1820s, though, when the 2nd Earl was making alterations to the house and his daughter Lady Harriet wrote to her brother just after he had returned from an eventful visit to Spain and Portugal:

> *I write you one line to say how delighted we are to hear you are safely arrived, and to strongly advise you not to come to Highclere which is in a very catchcold state no windows closing and the passages open to the new unfinished rooms and nothing would be so unfortunate as if you begin your residence in England by a bad cold.*

She added that their sister Lady Emily and her husband Philip Pusey

> *arrived yesterday and the cold of the unfinished rooms gave him a toothache so that he has been in his room ever since and I write to guard you against such a calamity... this will be a beautiful house when completed.*

Sixty years later, the 4th Earl did in fact install a heating system through some of the State Rooms – the Library, Saloon and Music Room – but it was not so effective that it interfered with the cool requirements of the indoor plants.

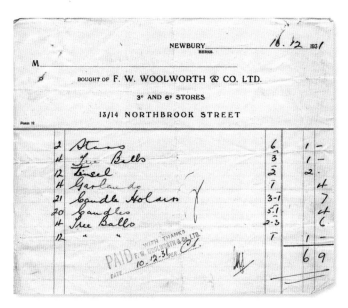

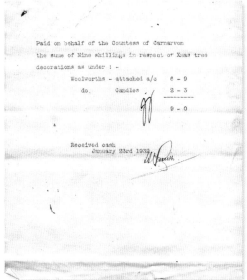

NEWBURY _____ 16.12 193/
BERKS.

M _____

BOUGHT OF **F. W. WOOLWORTH & CO. LTD.**

3ᵈ AND 6ᵈ STORES

13/14 NORTHBROOK STREET

Paid on behalf of the Countess of Carnarvon
the sum of Nine shillings in respect of Xmas tree
decorations as under : -

Woolworths - attached a/c   6 - 9

do.   Candles ,   2 - 3
                        ----
                          9 - 0

Received cash
January 23rd 1932

The heady scent of the narcissi in bloom can be almost overpowering, but it does work very well in one of the larger State Rooms, where the sheer space ensures it does not overwhelm. The stems of the narcissi and hyacinths all need some support from green canes and string to keep them upright. We tend to plant the hyacinth bulbs outside after they have flowered, with a little bone meal at the bottom of the hole to encourage them to take. Then we snip off the flower spire but leave the leaves alone to die down and replenish the bulb, so that they will come back to provide welcome glimpses of colour in the Wood of Goodwill in winter months.

Another much-admired Christmas plant is the poinsettia, which is now included in most Christmas decorations and displays. Native to Mexico, the small shrub with star-shaped leaf patterns called *la Flor de Nochebuena*, or Holy Night (Christmas Eve) flower, was originally known for its sap, which helped to cure fevers, and its leaves, which made a purple dye. In 1828, Joel R. Poinsett (1779–1851), the first US ambassador to Mexico, introduced the plant to the Bartram's Garden, a botanic garden and arboretum in Philadelphia. He probably never would have guessed that, fast forward almost two hundred years, the poinsettia, named after him, would become the UK's most popular flowering plant, with more than 70 million sold nationwide each year.

ABOVE
Receipts for Christmas
decorations from
the early 1930s

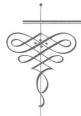

CHAPTER FIVE

THE CHRISTMAS TREE

❄ FEW SIGHTS ARE MORE ❄
WELCOMING ON A DARK WINTER EVENING

THAN THE TWINKLING LIGHTS ON A TREE, LIT AND decorated; it is the one thing that, above all, says Christmas. It greets friends and family and it gives a home to the presents piled underneath it, and, if it is real, lends a wonderful scent to the room.

NOSTALGIC, FULL OF HOPE AND SPARKLE, WE ALL LOOK forward to setting up our Christmas tree at Highclere, the one that is the focal point of our festive decorations. There is something reassuring about digging out scuffed family decorations – our own and those that friends have given us over the years. The tree in the Saloon is a real feature for our guests and visitors at Highclere, and something that they look out for – not just because of the spectacular scale of it but also the thought that we put into its decoration.

The tradition of decorating a Christmas tree was introduced to Britain by George III's wife, Queen Charlotte, but it really became popular after a drawing appeared in *The London Illustrated News* in December 1848 of Queen Victoria, her husband Prince Albert and their children gathered around their Christmas tree. Like Queen Charlotte, Prince Albert was German and the 'Weihnachtsbaum' (Christmas tree) was very much a part of his culture. The infamous sketch shows the Christmas tree at Windsor Castle, decorated with wax candles, glass figures and baubles, with the royal princes and princesses gathered around, their eyes lighting on the toys at its base.

Today, of course, most of us don't risk real candles on a tree, and instead we light them more conventionally with tiny sparkling electric lights, and our decorations have evolved from the earliest apples, nuts and coloured-paper ornaments, the Victorian glass baubles and tin figures to the present-day trends for tinsel and less-breakable plastic and metal baubles. Although traditionally Christmas trees were not brought into the house until Christmas Eve and were then removed on Twelfth Night, these dates have moved somewhat over the years, and some people today will start this period at the beginning of Advent or even on the American holiday of Thanksgiving, in late November. Contemporary agreement remains, however, that to keep a tree in the house later than Twelfth Night is considered unlucky.

PREVIOUS PAGE
Highclere's Christmas tree,
in pride of place in the Saloon,
the heart of the house

ABOVE
Queen Victoria's Christmas
tree at Windsor Castle,
as shown in *The Illustrated
London News*

DECORATING THE TREE

THE FIRST DAY OF DECEMBER IS WHEN WE ALL LEAP into action with the trees. Officially, 1 December is known as Saint Eligius' Day. St Eligius devoted his life to others through both practical talents (engineering and metalwork) and diplomacy, making him the perfect saint for 'Operation Christmas Tree'.

Standing in front of the Castle, outside the familiarly heavy, ingrained doors, the nose of the tractor emerges into view down the drive. It makes its way carefully between the two pale stone gateposts of Castle Lodge and drives towards us, before swinging around to ensure the trailer is parallel and as near to the front door as possible.

The tree in the trailer is a Norway spruce, still closely furled in its netting. This is the traditional tree chosen by Prince Albert for Queen Victoria, and the type given each year to Trafalgar Square by the people of Norway as a mark of friendship and a thank you for Britain's help in World War Two. As a child, I was taken to London to see that tree being set up; the ceremony, band and choir was a heartwarming start to Christmas. This idea of better times is also reflected at the Rockefeller Center, in New York, where, initially as a symbol of hope and optimism during the dire financial and economic times of the 1929 crash, another famous Christmas tree is erected each year.

Highclere's grand tree for the Saloon comes from a local supplier and is cut down just two days earlier, then left on the trailer in one of our barns to allow it to dry off. Mindful of Diana, our head housekeeper, who looks after everything inside the Castle so carefully and who will be at the sharp end, both literally and metaphorically, of this enormous tree, we try to keep the trail of needles and general outside detritus to the minimum.

Getting an extremely heavy twenty-foot tree into such a fragile and important building is a challenge in itself. Great care has to be taken that none of the stonework is damaged, let alone the leather wall hangings and branched candelabra lamps in the Saloon. The only way to do this is with an enormous amount of manpower...

The gardeners arrive to help, alongside Simon, Tom and Terry from the farm. John comes down from the office and lines up with David Hilton, our joiner, who has made the remarkable work of art that is the tree stand, which holds it steady and secure. The stand is a work of intricate and ingenious craftsmanship, made entirely from used floorboards from a cottage that was being renovated in the Park. It is beautifully constructed to include clamps to ensure the tree is held straight – a fitting piece of engineering for St Eligius' Day.

ABOVE
St Eligius of Noyen, in an
18th-century Dutch engraving

RIGHT
Highclere's tree, grown nearby
and carefully selected, arrives
at the Castle

BUYING YOUR TREE

If you have the choice of buying a real tree, first gauge the height that you can accommodate, then take the time to choose one that has a nice shape and is in good condition. The needles should be moist and bright green – crush them and see if they smell, or if, when you shake the tree gently, many needles fall off. We have, in the past, unwittingly bought trees that have been cut down far too early, which almost immediately began to drop their needles. On one year in particular, the main tree for the Saloon was so poor we had to remove it and start all over again.

As Terry undoes the trailer straps, Luis appears with his team from banqueting, ever enthusiastic and noisy, if more used to the art of setting the table. Amidst much banter and laughter, with the men lining up on either side of the trailer, the tree is lifted off, carried into the Saloon and laid down on sheets that have been spread out to protect the carpet. John carries on a running commentary about living the dream at Highclere and is this tree the right size? It is supposed to be eighteen to twenty-two feet, but I am never sure whether that includes the topmost part, which always seems a little bare.

Discussion meanders on about the height of the tree whilst the ropes are readied and, as the branches are loosened out, the Christmas fairies – both in the human form of Sally and the decorative tree version – make their appearance. Sally and the gift-shop girls whirl around the tree, attaching decorations to the topmost part whilst it is easily accessible. However, the three-legged construction of the stand means that the tree pivots as it is hauled upright, so the fairy on the top, which because of the height of the tree has to be fixed on whilst it is still prone, has to be attached at a precise angle to ensure it faces forward once the tree is up. Cue much learned discussion from the men about the degree of rotational swivel – all of which is ignored by Sally and her team.

My husband waits on the gallery landing above with Simon, our farm manager, ready to haul on the ropes to pull the tree upright. I am, naturally, to be found hauling on a rope against my husband to stop the tree crashing into the leather wall hangings. With much debate and loud instruction, the tree is slowly winched into position and starts to settle. The base invariably needs easing around, but as the branches unfurl and the tree warms in the heat of the house, releasing that unmistakable green fragrance, we declare a well-earned break and stop for soup and sausage rolls.

Within a short time, Luis and Matthew have brought out the tallest of ladders with accompanying mats on which to stand them, and Sally and her gift-shop elves become the lead organisers. Each year more decorations are sourced, bought or made, and the lightweight but ungainly boxes of those that have been stored from previous years are carefully refined. Sally's team make numerous journeys up and down the Red Stairs, to retrieve the boxes from storage on the third floor, more than earning their mince pies and cups of tea! The different colours and types are then laid out on trestle tables and the plan begins to take shape.

Sally tends to stand towards the back of the Saloon, directing operations in a commanding voice. Luis, Matthew and myself are sent up the ladders with long sticks with hooks on to enable us to reach the branches, whilst the

GIVE YOUR TREE THE BEST CHANCE OF SURVIVAL

Leave the tree in the netting that wraps up the branches until it is well installed in its receptacle in your home. If you can, take a saw and carefully make a small cut into the base of the trunk, then stand and wedge it in with some water so that it can have a good drink. Only then should you release the netting and let the branches drop and settle before you decorate it. Keep the lights away from the base of the tree when you set them in place, and remember to turn them off at night when you all go to bed.

gift-shop ladies wait below to hand out the appropriate decorations. First, two sets of white lights are draped around the tree before the decorations – from baubles to little figures – are hung in place. 'Just a little to the right, Matthew,' says Sally, before repeating, 'to the right, Matthew,' and then again the slightly more resigned, 'no, Matthew, that would be your other right,' as she struggles with her workforce and their slightly not-as-serious-as-they-should-be attitude.

After about two hours the tree is beginning to take shape. Just as everyone's energy is starting to wane, my husband reappears to pass judgement and have a cup of tea. With further scrutiny and incidental adjustments, we declare the job well done and toast it as such with mulled wine. I hope St Eligius would approve of our efforts and teamwork.

With the floor sheets removed and the boxes of leftover decorations back in storage, we leave Diana and her housekeeping team to return the Saloon to its stately order, with clean carpets and polished floors.

Sally begins work on the staircase, winding the garland down the banister rail, attaching it with wide red ribbons and hooking in extra bunches of decorations to form swags before eventually calling it a day.

The further twenty smaller trees which line the front drive, the ten more six- to eight-foot trees for the courtyard, the wreaths for the front door, the mantelpiece decorations and table decorations, can all wait for another day.

A LITTLE MORE HISTORY

THE CHRISTMAS TREE OWES ITS TWINKLING LIGHTS TO a story from five hundred years ago. A tall broad man dressed in a thick long coat, wide-brimmed hat pulled down, was walking home through the woods in Germany. He was called Martin Luther, in honour of St Martin's Day, on which he was baptised in 1483. It was perhaps a portent, given his future role in the reformation of the church, that he joined the church on the first day of Advent! He thought how beautifully the stars sparkled through the trees, so he cut down a tree and took it home to share with his wife. He carried it inside and during the evening tied small candles onto the branches, which he lit, saying they were symbols of the beautiful Christmas sky.

Just like the stars that sparkled through the dark green boughs of Luther's original trees, so further ways of adding twinkling light developed. The word tinsel is derived from the Latin word *scintilla*, which means a spark, and this festive decoration was originally made from real shredded silver leaf – which must have been very beautiful but also more than a little expensive! These days we have every permutation of light and sparkle on our trees, making it almost impossible to choose between them.

Another fable brings an even older tradition into the theme, mixing the fir with the Paradise tree to produce a tree decorated with apples, representing the Tree of Knowledge in the Garden of Eden. So from inventing the Christmas tree, Germany then led the way in manufacturing beautiful ornaments with which to decorate it, beginning with carvings of apples and birds by local craftsmen. These designs then progressed to miniature wooden toys and beautiful hand-blown and painted glass baubles.

By the end of the nineteenth century, as thousands of families followed the lead of their Queen, Victoria, the growing popularity of Christmas trees led to the manufacture of decorations such as painted figures made from tin, which were produced in great numbers and thus were available to all. Interestingly, the angels for the top of the tree were first made in doll factories. In fact, it was Christmas decorations that propelled the fortune of American retailer F.W. Woolworth, who, from 1880, imported baubles into the USA, apparently selling $25-million worth a year.

Martin Luther, in an engraving by Lucas Cranach the Elder from 1520

LADY CARNARVON'S CREAM OF JERUSALEM ARTICHOKE SOUP

Jerusalem artichokes are easy to grow – and in fact can be problematic as they spread very successfully. They were not first grown in Jerusalem, as the name suggests, but likely are so-called because early Italian settlers in America dubbed them *girasol* (sunflowers) because their blooms look like sunflowers.

I do not think these root vegetables are included in our diets nearly enough. They have a lovely nutty flavour and are good for our digestion and gut, so if you see them, buy them because they are delicious simply roasted in the oven in butter and herbs. Any left over can be sliced when cool and added to a salad. This is Paul's recipe for a warming soup.

PREPARATION TIME 20 mins   COOKING TIME 50 mins   SERVES 6–8

INGREDIENTS

75g (3oz) butter

8 banana shallots, chopped

1·5kg (3¼lb) Jerusalem artichokes, peeled and chopped to roughly the same size

2 garlic cloves, thinly sliced

2 bay leaves

2 sprigs of thyme

1·5 litres (2½ pints) vegetable stock

600ml (1 pint) double cream

Ground white pepper and salt, to taste

METHOD

§   Place the butter in a heavy-based pan over a medium heat. Add the shallots and cook until they are soft and going transparent, which should take 5–6 minutes. Add the artichokes, garlic, bay leaves and thyme and sauté until the artichokes start to slightly colour, 8–10 minutes.

§   Add the vegetable stock, bring up to the boil, then simmer over a low heat for around 20 minutes or until the artichokes are completely cooked. Pierce with a sharp knife or skewer to make sure.

§   Take the mixture off the heat and blitz with a stick blender until completely smooth. Stir in the cream and season to taste, then return to a low heat and simmer for a further 10 minutes or until it reaches your preferred thickness.

§   Great with sliced brown bread and unsalted butter.

MRS MACKIE'S HAM

Mrs Mackie was the Castle cook here circa 1930, and this is her recipe for ham:

Soak the ham for 14 hours.

Place in a huge black cooking pot and cover with a gallon of old beer. Cook gently for several hours.

Skin the ham, score and stick with cloves, cover with brown sugar and a small bottle of champagne.

Put in an oven and continually baste until the sugar has caramelised and the ham has turned a delicious brown in colour.

HIGHCLERE HAM

We still often use and enjoy Mrs Mackie's recipe today, but an alternative is to use cider instead of beer, as apples and pork/ham are such a good combination.

A proper ham is an excellent centre piece for a lunch during Christmas and my family's cook, Queenie, used to make parsley sauce to serve with it, along with well-mashed potato, peas and carrots. It was hopefully far too large and could then be used cold or in other subsequent dishes.

PREPARATION TIME 10 mins   COOKING TIME 9 hrs, plus resting   SERVES 20+ portions

INGREDIENTS

1 large onion, quartered
1 carrot, chopped
3 bay leaves
Sprigs of parsley and thyme
6kg (13lb) unsmoked ham
1·5 litres (2½ pints) cider
3 tbsp golden syrup
1 tbsp mustard powder
Handful of cloves

METHOD

§   Preheat the oven to 240°C/475°F/Gas mark 8.

§   Spread all the vegetables and herbs in a large roasting tin to make a trivet and place the ham on top. Pour over the cider and wrap the whole pan in a double layer of tin foil.

§   Put the roasting tin into the oven for 20 minutes, then turn the heat down to 120°C/240°F/Gas mark 1 and cook for 8 hours. Alternatively, transfer it to the lower, cooler Aga oven and leave to cook overnight.

§   Remove the ham from the oven and carefully remove the foil. Transfer the ham to a chopping board and discard the vegetables and any leftover cider.

§   Peel away the top layer of skin and score the fat in a criss-cross pattern.

§   Line the roasting tin with foil and return the ham to it.

§   Mix the golden syrup and mustard powder together and brush over the ham. Stick the cloves into the fat where the lines cross.

§   Increase the heat of the oven to 200°C/400°F/Gas mark 6 and when hot put in the ham to bake for 30–40 minutes, until it has taken on a deep golden colour. Remove from the oven and allow to rest for at least 20 minutes before serving.

GINGERBREAD

Gingerbread biscuits have been part of our cooking heritage for centuries. The flat sweet biscuit is easy to mould and shape, whether into houses or people or animals, iced and studded with currants and other decorations. Nuremberg, in Germany, considered itself the Gingerbread Capital in 1395 and its medieval bakers used curved boards to create elaborate designs.

Apparently Queen Elizabeth had some made to resemble the dignitaries at her court, to be served at festivals that came to be known as Gingerbread Fairs. The gingerbread biscuits became known as 'fairings'. Given we grew up in Cornwall, we rather support the Cornish claim to 'Cornish Fairings', which became famous around the country when a Cornish manufacturer started selling them by mail order in 1886. The company is still proudly baking biscuits today.

PREPARATION TIME 10 mins   COOKING TIME 20 mins   MAKES at least 20 biscuits

INGREDIENTS

225g (8oz) plain flour,
   plus extra for dusting
1 tsp salt
1 tsp bicarbonate of soda
1½ tsp ground ginger
1 tsp ground cinnamon
100g (3½oz) unsalted
   butter
100g (3½oz) soft brown
   sugar
100g (3½oz) golden syrup

TO DECORATE
Icing
Currants
Dried cranberries

METHOD

§   Take your dry ingredients – flour, salt, bicarbonate of soda, ginger and cinnamon – and sift into a large mixing bowl.

§   In a heavy-based pan over a medium heat, heat the butter, sugar and syrup, stirring, until the sugar has dissolved. Remove from the heat and pour into the dry mixture, stirring with a spoon until you form a dough.

§   Roll out the dough on a lightly floured surface and cut with your shaped cutter; we normally aim for about 5mm (¼ inch) thick but don't over work the dough.

§   Place the cut-outs on a baking tray lined with baking paper and bake for 10–15 minutes until nicely golden in colour. When cooked, remove from the oven and allow to cool on a cooling rack.

§   When they are cooled, have a fun time with the children (or adults behaving like children) decorating them with icing, currants or dried cranberries.

HIGHCLERE MINCE PIES

Mincemeat and mince pies have been part of British cookery for centuries and did originally contain meat, though now the only meat in the dish is in the beef suet. These are a perfect restorative snack while decorating the tree. If you don't have time to make your own mincemeat, very good versions are available in the shops.

PREPARATION TIME **40 mins, plus chilling** COOKING TIME **20–25 mins** MAKES **12**

INGREDIENTS

FOR THE MINCEMEAT

225g (8oz) suet (you can use beef or vegetarian suet)

225g (8oz) Bramley apples, peeled, cored and chopped

125g (4½oz) candied peel, chopped

225g (8oz) sultanas

225g (8oz) raisins

225g (8oz) currants

175g (6oz) demerara sugar

1 tsp mixed spice

Zest and juice of 1 orange

60ml (2½ fl oz) Cognac

FOR THE PASTRY

225g (8oz) cold butter, diced, plus extra for greasing

350g (12oz) plain flour, plus extra for dusting

100g (3½oz) caster sugar

Pinch of salt

Grated zest and a squeeze of juice from ½ orange (optional)

1 egg, beaten

Icing sugar, for dusting

METHOD

TO MAKE THE MINCEMEAT

§   Mix all the ingredients together in a large mixing bowl.

§   Spoon into sterilised jars (see page 308) and store in a cool dark place. It improves with age, but can be used straight away.

TO MAKE THE PIES

§   Preheat the oven to 180°C/350°F/Gas mark 4.

§   To make the pastry, rub the butter into the flour, then mix in the caster sugar and a pinch of salt. Add the orange zest and juice, if using. I recommend you do – it adds an utterly delicious extra dimension!

§   Roll out the pastry on a lightly floured work surface and cut out twelve circles for the lids and twelve slightly larger circles for the bases of the pies. Place the bases in a greased twelve-hole Yorkshire pudding tray.

§   Spoon 280g (10oz) of the mincemeat into the pies. Top the pies with the lids, pressing the edges gently together to seal and run around the edge with the tines of a fork.

§   Brush the tops of the pies with the beaten egg, then bake in the oven for 20–25 minutes until golden. Leave to cool in the tin for 5 minutes, then remove from the tin and allow to cool on a wire rack.

§   Serve lightly dusted with icing sugar.

MEDIEVAL MINCE PIE

Many medieval recipes combined sweet and savoury ingredients, and pies were no exception. Sweetness often came courtesy of honey or dried fruits, as sugar was not widely available. Along with spices such as saffron and ginger, dried fruits such as figs and dates had to be imported into the country. Due to the inclusion of these expensive ingredients, spiced pies were not for every day; they were only served on important feast days such as Easter or Christmas (which were both preceded by fasts).

It's hard to know exactly when meat was dropped from the mince pie. *Mrs Beeton's Book of Household Management* (1861) originally gave two recipes for mincemeat – one with and one without meat. This recipe was originally published in *A book of cookrye Very necessary for all such as delight therin*, printed by Edward Allde (1591).

PREPARATION TIME 15 mins   COOKING TIME 1 hr 50 mins   SERVES 8–10

INGREDIENTS

FOR THE FILLING
700g (1½lb) lean mutton
  or beef mince
100g (3½oz) suet
½ tsp ground cloves
1 tsp ground mace
½ tsp black pepper
A pinch of saffron
50g (2oz) raisins
50g (2oz) currants
50g (2oz) stoned prunes,
  chopped

FOR THE PASTRY
450g (1lb) plain flour, plus
  extra for dusting
2 tsp salt
100g (3½oz) lard
150ml (5fl oz) water
4 tbsp milk

FOR THE GLAZE
1 tbsp butter
1 tbsp sugar
1 tbsp rosewater

METHOD

§   Preheat the oven to 220°C/425°F/Gas mark 7 and grease and line a 20cm (8 inch) deep loose-bottomed tin.

§   Mix together all the ingredients for the filling in a large mixing bowl and work well with your hands to combine. Keep to one side.

§   To make the pastry, sift the flour and salt together into a large mixing bowl and make a well in the centre. Heat the lard, water and milk together in a saucepan until boiling, then pour into the flour well. Quickly beat the mixture together with a spoon to form a soft dough, and knead until smooth on a lightly floured board.

§   Cut off a quarter of the pastry, and keep covered until required to make the lid. Mould the larger piece of pastry into the tin to form the base and sides of the pie.

§   Pack in the meat, trying to avoid creating any airholes, and dampen the edges of the pie wall. Roll out the remaining pastry to make a lid and firmly press into place. Trim the edges, using any surplus pastry for decoration, and cut a hole in the centre of the lid.

§   Place the pie onto a lipped baking sheet, to catch any juices that may escape, and bake for 15 minutes. Then reduce the oven temperature to 180°C/350°F/Gas mark 4 and cook for a further 1¼ hours. Take out of the oven and carefully remove the sides of the tin, brush the pie all over with the glaze and return to the oven for a further 15 minutes to brown.

§   Remove from the oven and allow to cool for 15 minutes on the tin base before transferring to a cooling rack to cool completely. Serve cold.

CHAPTER SIX

GIFTS & SHOPPING

❄ WHATEVER YOU THINK ❄

ABOUT TODAY'S POSSIBLE OVER-COMMERCIALISATION OF CHRISTMAS, THE GIVING and receiving of gifts continues to play a central role in most people's celebrations. The Bible tells us of the wise men who brought gifts of myrrh, frankincense and gold to the baby Jesus – not actually at his birth but sometime later. That symbolic date of the Epiphany is now set as 6 January, although most of us keep our gift-giving to 25 December.

WE ASSUME THERE WERE THREE MAGI AS THERE WERE three gifts, but there could have been many more of these wise men, and they may collectively have brought the gifts narrated in the gospel of Matthew. They were called wise men and then kings, which of course assumes that kings (or those in charge) are wise, which is itself something of a leap of logic. In a rather modern way, the three Magi – Balthazar, Melchior and Caspar – have traditionally been described as coming from different ethnic groups and being diverse in heritage.

However, their choice of gifts was very specific: gold, which at any time is useful, but more importantly is a symbol of the kingship of the baby Jesus; frankincense, a symbol of holiness and righteousness with medicinal and healing qualities; and myrrh, again, a plant that heals wounds but was also used for embalming – thus at Jesus's birth it was also pointing to his death.

CHRISTMAS MARKETS

WHERE YOU HAVE GIFTS, YOU ALSO HAVE SHOPPING. These days we are spoilt for choice, but historically you relied on Christmas markets, the most famous of which are probably those in Germany. Many of these have been taking place for at least four hundred years, and with entertainments, carousels, bell ringing, stalls with ovens baking potatoes and sausages, special cakes dusted with icing, and tree decorations, they are an experience to enjoy. A favourite recipe, if only for the name, is *Himmel und Erde* (Heaven and Earth), which consists of black pudding (or sausages), fried onions, mashed potatoes and apple sauce. Apples are from the tree (heaven), but of course they are also the forbidden fruit, thus leading us away from heaven, and potatoes are from the earth – 'earth apples' in German.

We hold our own fair at Highclere; it is nothing like the magnificent German ones but at its heart it is still about gifts and food and people gathering together. It, too, has become an annual tradition. I have always liked Winston Churchill's words: 'We make a living by what we get. We make a life by what we give,' and our fair raises money for two very good local causes: the church and the Air Ambulance.

The fair also acts as the deadline for the Castle decorations, which must be finished down to the last bow before we welcome local stallholders who have been booked months ahead. They arrive laden with a wide range of food and drink to sell within the Castle, outside and in a marquee, bringing clothing, jewellery, books and cards, warm hats and soothing bath oils, and pampering lotions to ward off winter winds. Diana, our housekeeper, rushes round with mats and cloths trying to ensure that nothing is damaged whilst making life as easy as possible for them all to set up. Space is often tight but they are remarkably good-humoured about it and all profess to love the atmosphere.

LEFT
The Highclere Castle
Christmas Fair in full swing

Outside amongst the Christmas trees in the courtyard, there is the unmistakable smell of roasting chestnuts, served with spicy mulled wine or a hot spiced apple drink to warm shoppers who venture to admire the carved wooden reindeer and tree decorations made from fallen Highclere wood. Paul, our chef, and his kitchen team have produced warming winter soups, mince pies, mulled wine, Christmas quiches and an assortment of cakes to serve throughout the day in the tearooms. Carol singers serenade our visitors, both inside and outside, making for a wonderfully festive, happy occasion.

We all pray for good weather – not only to preserve the fun in the courtyard but to help preserve the car parking, too. There is only a limited amount of hard-standing parking at the Castle, because we are surrounded by beautiful grass parkland, which can make parking in bad weather a little tricky. However, the journey to the Castle is nothing by comparison to the journey of the Magi, which was neither easy, nor pleasant, nor safe.

T.S. Eliot's much-read poem *The Journey of the Magi* sets the scene:

A cold coming we had of it,
Just the worst time of the year
For a journey, and such a long journey
The ways deep and the weather sharp,
The very dead of winter....

ABOVE
Decorations made from
fallen trees from the
Highclere Estate

RIGHT
Lady Carnarvon peruses the
Christmas decorations for sale
at the Christmas Fair

The poet wrote it very quickly:

*I had been thinking about it in church... and when I got home I opened
a half-bottle of Booth's Gin, poured myself a drink, and began to write.
By lunchtime, the poem, and the half-bottle of gin, were both finished.*

Far from the journey through wintry landscapes of earlier centuries, the
press of visitors arriving today, in cosy coats and hats, instead make their
way through shopping stalls – although the gifts they buy may bear some
resemblance to those of old, with perhaps some gold jewellery, a perfumed
bath oil or some Highclere Castle Gin to aid celebrations.

All quite orderly and organised at the start of the day, as the list of presents
to buy gets adjusted and altered and the place gets busier, so it becomes a bit
more higgledy-piggledy. Is it the right thing? Have they missed something?
Is there a bargain or perhaps a present for oneself? Then, weighed down
with piles of Christmas shopping, visitors and guests finally return to their
cars, aided with much goodwill by Paul McTaggart and the car-parking team.

The dogs think it is Christmas already because there is such a good
chance of extra pickings. I think it is Christmas already because I don't
have to go shopping – it is all here.

Get in the Christmas spirit
as early as you like with our
GIN COCKTAILS
PAGE 111

W R A P P I N G

PART OF THE FUN OF GIVING OR RECEIVING A GIFT IS
the sense of anticipation and curiosity for both giver and receiver, of
wondering what the wrapped gift is and whether it will be appreciated as
much as you hope it will be. This Christmas tradition of wrapping presents
is rather recent, and the gifts in the sketches of Queen Victoria and her
family by their Christmas tree are clearly shown unwrapped.

Wrapping paper, however, is not new. It was first documented in Ancient
China, where paper, as opposed to papyrus or parchment, was first invented
in the second century BC by a court official called Cai Lun. Monetary gifts
were wrapped in paper forming an envelope called a *chih pao*, which were
then distributed by the Chinese court to government officials. Papermaking
was kept a secret by the Chinese for centuries, but it spread to the Islamic
world in the eighth century AD.

By the eleventh century it had reached Europe, with manufacturing
becoming more refined by the use of water mills in Spain in the thirteenth
century. It wasn't until the nineteenth century, when wood-based papers
were invented, that wrapping paper became much more affordable.

The wrapping paper we use today, however, is a relatively recent invention.
One hundred years ago, when the Granthams might have lived at 'Downton

A quick and easy soup
to warm you after a hard
morning's wrapping:
BEETROOT SOUP
PAGE 106

Abbey', gifts at any time of year were more usually wrapped in tissue paper or brown paper and string. Before that, cloth was mostly used.

The ability to manufacture reasonably priced, easily foldable paper did not appear until the early 1900s in the USA, but challenges remained in gift-wrapping, as adhesive tape was not invented until the 1930s. Soon after that, all presents were wrapped and the art of wrapping became a lifestyle choice, with articles on how to do it in magazines and books. Today, for some, it has even become part of the present itself, with crystal-encrusted paper available at £1,000 a sheet and specialist 'international gift-wrapping consultants' who will wrap your gifts in handmade papers studded with jewels costing thousands.

Conversely, in the face of this vast commercialisation, there is also a small but growing movement away from disposable wrapping, as people start to worry about its impact on the environment. Scientists have recently estimated that the USA alone generates an extra five million tonnes of waste over the Christmas period, most of which is wrapping paper and shopping bags. The problem is that a lot of Christmas wrapping paper, in particular, cannot be recycled as it is decorated with foil or glitter.

The most mundane things can be surprisingly effective as wrapping paper. I remember one Christmas when one of my friends was feeling

particularly impoverished and decided that wrapping paper was not a good use of her budget. So instead she wrapped all her presents in pages of the *Financial Times* newspaper, which is a rather fetching shade of salmon pink. Finished with black ribbon bows, the parcels looked effortlessly stylish and, of course, were eco-friendly.

HOW TO WRAP

TODAY, IT COULD BE SAID THAT THERE ARE THOSE WHO wrap and those who use gift bags. According to industry research, Americans today spend approximately $3.2 billion each year on wrapping paper and gift bags, with gift bags outstripping paper as the wrap of choice. For those of us who are not naturally deft, wrapping can be both an expensive and frustrating experience, but the trick is to be organised and then to practise.

Get everything you need together before you start – it takes away much of the element of frustration if you are not continually searching for things. This will include the gifts (obviously), paper, scissors, adhesive tape, ribbon, gift tags, pen and any other decorative items you may wish to use.

Work out how much paper you will need – the height of the paper needs to be enough to wrap round the item plus a 2·5–7·5cm/1–3 inch overlap. However, you also need to consider the quality of the paper you are using. Cheaper papers are, by their nature, thinner, which means they rip more easily, therefore you are likely to need more. They can also be a bit see-through, which again means that you may need more. Thicker papers don't tear but they can be harder to fold neatly and sometimes need better or more tape to hold them down – or you can use wool or ribbons to hold the parcel together instead of tape, then the paper can be re-used for years to come.

Perhaps think about a more environmentally friendly alternative, such as scraps of fabric or recycled paper. Or just avoid glittery, non-biodegradable paper. If you are using fabric, consider how you are going to fix it together.

Sort out your ribbon, if you are using it. Wire-edged ribbon makes beautiful neat bows but is expensive, whilst satin ribbon looks lovely but has to be knotted tightly to ensure it doesn't slip, otherwise you can just use ordinary ribbon, which is less substantial but perhaps easier to tie.

Add in any other decoration you feel like using – little bunches of artificial berries, tiny ornaments, pine cones or flowers.

Last but not least, write the gift tag and attach it securely so that there is no muddle about the recipient.

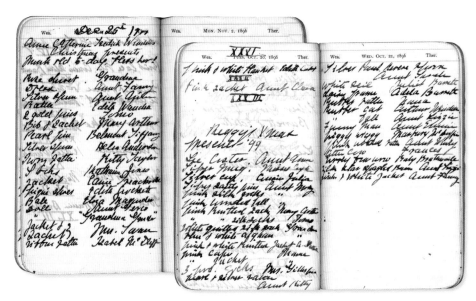

GIVING THANKS

APART FROM GIFTS TO FAMILY AND WHICHEVER OF OUR
friends are staying, I also give small presents to the office, estate and farm
teams here. My husband used to give whiskey to some of his team, but I
gathered not all liked whiskey and I also realised that, as Highclere's teams
expanded in number, not everyone received gifts.

I have happily tried to take account of both challenges and begin with
such good intentions of lists, but always end up panicked and nearly late.
Some presents are carefully wrapped and then, as time shortens, I use
Highclere paper-handled bags and tissue paper.

It is a way of saying a small thank you, whether to gardeners, or shepherds,
banqueting kitchen, office, security, housekeeping, keepers, electricians or
joiners. As Christmas approaches and the task grows and bags are lined
up around the floor, I normally find someone's gift is wine but they do not
drink, or other poor choices, and so Geordie is dispatched in a flurry to
buy more festive tins of biscuits or cheese.

The archives have records, including from the time of Almina, the 5th
Countess, noting gifts to tenants (who normally worked at the Castle) and
household staff. At this time of year many received shawls, warm vests
or other clothes, and throughout the rest of the year anyone who was ill
might be given wine, Bovril or Liebig's Extract of Meat, so it seems we have
simply returned, after a fashion, to the same tradition.

THE HIGHCLERE CHRISTMAS QUIZ

PART 2

H I S T O R Y

1/ The influenza pandemic that swept around the globe during and after the First World War is estimated to have killed how many people worldwide?

2/ The first Earl of Carnarvon died fighting for Charles I at the First Battle of Newbury, but what was the date and year of this battle?

3/ What year did Geoffrey de Havilland make his first flight?

4/ Sir John A. Macdonald, who visited Highclere, became the first Prime Minister of The Province of Canada, but in what year?

5/ The 'boy king' Tutankhamun acceded to the throne at the age of nine in 1336 BC. During which Dynasty was he Pharaoh? What was the name of this period in Egyptian history?

6/ How old was Tutankhamun when he died?

7/ Neville Chamberlain visited Downton Abbey, and had dinner with the Crawley family, but for which party did he stand?

8/ Neville Chamberlain became Prime Minister in 1937, but from whom did he take over, and why?

9/ The English Civil War was a series of conflicts from 1642–1651 between Royalists and Parliamentarians, but what are the two sides known as more colloquially?

10/ The third Earl of Carnarvon, Henry Herbert was elected a fellow of the Royal Society in 1841. Can you name any two of the five members of the royal family who are currently nominated 'Royal Fellows'?

W H O   S A I D . . .

11/ 'Can you see anything?' ... and who replied 'Yes, wonderful things'?

12/ 'Principles are like prayers; noble of course, but awkward at a party'?

H I G H C L E R E   T O D A Y

13/ How many dogs do Lord and Lady Carnarvon have?

14/ What type of oil is produced by the farm at Highclere?

ANSWERS

1/ 50-100 million   2/ 20 September 1643   3/ 1910   4/ 1857   5/ 18th Dynasty; New Kingdom/New Empire Period   6/ 19   7/ The Conservatives   8/ Stanley Baldwin, who retired   9/ Cavaliers and Roundheads   10/ The Duke of Edinburgh, The Duke of Kent, The Princess Royal, The Duke of Cambridge   11/ Lord Carnarvon and Howard Carter, opening the tomb of Tutankhamun   12/ The Dowager Countess   13/ 9   14/ Rapeseed

BEETROOT SOUP
(BORSCHT)

Whilst this soup looks impressive, it is quick and easy to make and the shocking-pink beetroot is a wonderful colour for Christmas. Beetroot has a long history; it was enjoyed by the Romans, and has also been used for food dyes. It is deep and earthy in flavour, and worthy, too, with strong health credentials – as a great source of fibre and minerals, including iron, potassium and manganese, which are essential for good health.

Whilst Paul may have good vegetable stock on hand, I am equally happy making this with tins of chicken consommé and, as ever, it is something that I can prepare ahead.

PREPARATION TIME **15 mins**   COOKING TIME **45 mins**   SERVES 6–8

INGREDIENTS

100g (3½oz) butter
1kg (2¼lb) red beetroot, peeled and chopped
2 onions, chopped
2 celery stalks, chopped
1 leek, chopped
2 large carrots, peeled and chopped
6 garlic cloves, finely sliced
2 litres (3½ pints) vegetable stock
Salt and pepper
Sour cream and dill, to garnish

METHOD

§   Melt the butter in a heavy-based pan over a medium heat. Add the beetroot, onion, celery, leek, carrots and garlic and sweat for 5 minutes, stirring often to avoid it taking on any colour. Add the vegetable stock and bring up to the boil before simmering for 30 minutes.

§   Blitz with a stick blender until completely smooth. Season to taste, then return to the heat and simmer for a further 10 minutes or until it reaches your preferred thickness.

§   Serve with a dollop of sour cream and garnish with dill.

GARLIC ROSEMARY FOCACCIA

For many centuries focaccia has had an association with Christmas Eve and Epiphany, although the bread has an even longer heritage, as it was baked by the Etruscans. It is in some ways a cross between bread and pizza, thus it is much loved by all the family. It is delicious cooked with rosemary and garlic sprinkled over it, and served with an olive oil dip or alongside a soup.

PREPARATION TIME 30 mins, plus proving time COOKING TIME 20–25 mins SERVES 10–12

INGREDIENTS

700g (1½lb) strong white
    bread flour
15g (½oz) dried yeast
20g (¾oz) salt
450ml (15fl oz) tepid water
40ml (1½fl oz) olive oil,
    plus extra for greasing
4 sprigs of rosemary,
    finely chopped
6 garlic cloves,
    finely chopped (or less,
    depending on your taste)
20g (¾oz) Maldon sea salt
Extra virgin olive oil

METHOD

§   Mix the flour, yeast and salt in a bowl with the tepid water until you form a dough. It should be soft but not sticky. Knead the dough on a clean worktop for 10–15 minutes.

§   Transfer to a clean, lightly-oiled mixing bowl, cover with cling film and leave to prove until it is doubled in size. This will take around an hour.

§   Line a 30 × 40cm (12 × 16 inch) baking tray with non-stick baking paper.

§   When the dough is ready, gently knock it back in the bowl before transferring it to the baking tray. Use your hands to press the dough out to fill the base of the tray. Cover with more cling film and leave to double in size again, about 45 minutes.

§   Preheat the oven to 220°C/425°F/Gas mark 7.

§   Mix together the olive oil, rosemary and garlic, and when the dough is ready, dip your fingertip into the oil and press dimples down into the dough, making sure they are prominent. Drizzle over the rest of the olive oil, rosemary and garlic.

§   Sprinkle over the sea salt then place the tray into the hot oven for 20–25 minutes until a deep golden brown.

§   Remove from the oven and drizzle over a little extra virgin olive oil.

§   This bread is fabulous on the day of cooking but it can also be used the next day sliced and toasted.

GIN COCKTAILS

HIGHCLERE CASTLE GIN COCKTAIL

INGREDIENTS

FOR THE THYME SYRUP
250ml (10fl oz) water
250g (9oz) caster sugar
10 sprigs of thyme

FOR EACH COCKTAIL
50ml (2fl oz) Highclere
   Castle Gin
25ml (1fl oz) thyme syrup
Ice, to serve
150ml (5fl oz) tonic water
Sprigs of thyme, to garnish
Pink grapefruit, sliced
   thinly and cut into thirds,
   to garnish

METHOD

§   To make the thyme syrup, add equal quantities of water and sugar into a saucepan over a medium heat, bring to a boil and stir until the sugar has dissolved.

§   Remove the pan from the heat and add the thyme sprigs. Let the syrup cool, then strain it through a sieve.

§   To make the cocktail, pour the gin and the syrup into a Copa de Balon glass filled with ice and stir.

§   Add the tonic water slowly and stir slowly.

§   Garnish with a thyme sprig and grapefruit slices.

WHITE LADY

The former Head Barman at The Savoy first introduced egg white to cocktails in the 1930s as he felt it bound together the elements of the drink to give a silkier finish. I rather like it, but our butler Luis says that bartenders today rarely use it. I must pop in to The Savoy to see if they are keeping the tradition alive.

INGREDIENTS

FOR EACH COCKTAIL
50ml (2fl oz)
   Highclere Castle Gin
25ml (1fl oz) Cointreau
15ml (½fl oz)
   fresh lemon juice
½ egg white (optional)
Ice
Lemon peel, to garnish

METHOD

§   If using egg white, pour all the ingredients into the shaker and shake (we call this a dry shake), then open, fill up with ice and shake again.

§   If you are leaving out the egg white, simply put all the ingredients into a shaker, fill it up with ice and shake it.

§   Pour into a classic Martini glass and garnish with the lemon peel.

CHAPTER SEVEN

TRADITIONS

☙ ONE OF THE CURIOUS ☙

ATTRIBUTES OF TRADITIONS IS THAT

THEY UNITE US, NOT JUST WITH OUR FRIENDS and family but also with the past and our ancestors. The nearest Anglo-Saxon word to tradition is *gesegen*, relating to sagas and storytelling (as does the German verb *sagen*). Anglo-Saxon poetry is the earliest extant in Europe and these long tales such as *The Wanderer*, tell of homecomings in bad weather and traditions of welcome and celebration binding communities together in tougher times.

IF WE WALKED SIX THOUSAND YEARS BACK IN TIME AT Highclere we would find a group of early settlers at the foot of Weald Setl (Beacon Hill). With homes and hearths, fields and livestock, they lived in a stable, agricultural society; working the lightly tilled land and watering the crops with good water from the chalk substrata (with calcium), growing wild hazelnuts for protein and trees for timber and firewood.

Across the fields they buried their dead in tumuli according to their traditions. They left no pictures nor textual script but might well have told stories of bravery and ghosts, handing down their customs and beliefs from generation to generation.

Outside, on clear frosty nights, as part of the endless search for the meaning and significance of existence, people used to see their lives and values reflected in stellar constellations.

Traditions give us a sense of order and safety, and Christmas is one rare time of year that can help foster cooperation amongst many countries, societies and communities. The overriding story at Christmas is, of course, that of Christ's birth, but other tales link us to pre-Christian roots, to northern tales set around Yule logs and the mythological character Nisse from Nordic folklore, to processions, rituals and stories of ghosts.

Many of the elements are similar – messages of rebirth and the hope of eternal peace – and meld together to give us the stories and beliefs that make up our own cultural beliefs at this time of year.

PREVIOUS PAGES
A cluster of white Poinsettias
in the North Library fireplace

ABOVE
Highclere Castle
illuminated by winter stars

The importance of traditions – of their roots and history – should never be underestimated. They give us comfort and reassurance, help to combat our innate fear of transience and instil a sense of timelessness.

THE YULE LOG

AS DECEMBER APPROACHES, TWO OF OUR TEAM, LUIS and Charlotte, become very industrious wood workers during their spare time. Rather than let good timber go to waste on the estate, we store it and, in this case, it is used to create Christmas tree decorations and small Yule logs.

Candles are set into the latter and the logs are decorated – they look charming, ready to sell to all enthusiastic Christmas visitors, if not those travelling onwards by plane.

In fact and fable, a Yule log was a huge log, a veritable block of timber, which was traditionally hauled into the hearth of each home before Christmas, whereupon stories were sung and children danced. Specially selected, it should remain alight throughout the Christmas period so that your ailments or mistakes could all be burned away.

Following the ritual of the Yule log would mean you could start afresh in the New Year, although, like any good story, there was a dark side: the Yule log should not on any account be allowed to go out or misfortune and death would come to the family.

The tradition continues that we should all save a piece of the Yule log with which to light next year's log, and on Christmas morning, something green, such as a leaf, should be brought into the home before anything is taken out. It is undoubtedly a very old tradition, and the word Yule, or Jul, remains at the heart of Scandinavian Christmases today. Jul celebrates the winter solstice, and the dark days of winter are especially intense in northern countries. Linked through common ancestry to Scandinavia, it is not hard to imagine our predecessors in the Bronze Age fort two miles south of the current Castle, lighting fires at this time as a symbol of the returning sun, as they sat before the tumuli they built for their dead.

Luis and Charlotte's logs are symbolic and a reminder of past gatherings and magic folklore, and signify it is time to light the candles, drink Yule ale and perhaps ask the cook in the house to make a chocolate yule log cake.

This cake, in the shape of a log, is usually baked in a large, shallow Swiss roll tin, which is layered with jam and cream, then rolled up to make a cylinder or log before being iced in dark chocolate on the outside. You can create the texture of bark by dragging a fork through the icing and dusting it with icing sugar for snow. It is usually decorated with a sprig of holly.

Our recipe for an indulgent
Christmas treat:
YULE LOG
PAGE 192

THE SPIRIT OF CHRISTMAS

EVEN IF THE BIRTH OF CHRIST HAS BEEN CELEBRATED
for over two thousand years, much of the spirit and traditions that we
take for granted in our Christmas celebrations today look back less than
two hundred years to the stories, morality and traditions created by the
pre-eminent Victorian novelist Charles Dickens.

His first novel was *The Pickwick Papers*, in which the eponymous hero
joins Mr Wardle and his family and friends to spend Christmas in the
country, telling each other ghost stories on Christmas Eve, drinking punch
(perhaps a version of mulled wine) and singing a carol. Past traditions had
been processions and rituals outside, but Charles Dickens brought the
celebration inside, into cosy evenings and the family home.

The colour of his stories stems from his own family experiences of
midwinter and Christmas as a child. He was born in Portsmouth, in southern
Hampshire, in 1812, two years before the Great Frost Fair, one of the coldest
years on record, when the Thames froze in London and there were stalls,
food, carnivals and horse racing on the snow-covered river. The following
years were also cold and snowy, and his memories were transformed into
the scenes and characters in his books – glowing illusions which still
transport us back to that era.

Whilst the Victorians did not invent ghost stories, the genre became very popular during that time. Many of these tales take place in the dark days of December, with Dickens's *A Christmas Carol* becoming one of the most famous. As the author's family grew in number, the central role of the wife and mother developed in both his life and his books. Thus, by the time he wrote *A Christmas Carol*, five years after *The Pickwick Papers*, Mrs Cratchit, 'flushed but smiling proudly' with her cooking, takes centre stage. The family live in London, under the smog of trains and work, they are not well off but have gathered together from their various worlds of work, returning home by train or on foot through the dirty, grey streets.

Unlike the country communities of the time, they have not invited friends to celebrate with them but are doing their best in their own home with little spare money. The old rural rhythm of life has changed with relentless urban working obligations, and consequently fewer days given as Christmas holiday, already a contrast to the scenes in *The Pickwick Papers*, where the reader is immersed in the generosity of the farming cycle in midwinter when, in the short cold days, very little could be achieved outside in the fields and orchards.

A Christmas Carol has a religious title and chapters called staves, recalling musical verses, but the Ghost of Christmas Present has a very different heritage. In description and illustration he harks back to a much older figure, a jolly green man, surrounded by greenery and feasting. The Green Man figure appears in many cultures and is found in carvings on churches, stones and barns, symbolising rebirth and the cycle of growth, from Roman mosaics to ancient headstones and even on a table in the Castle.

Dickens's version, however, was the spirit who 'stood by sick beds... in misery's every refuge ... and [who] taught Scrooge his precepts'. Ultimately,

An intriguing Victorian
recipe from the
Castle archives:
1860s SCONE/CAKE
PAGE 130

A Christmas Carol is a story of redemption and of gifting from the more prosperous to the less well-off. Equally it was published at a time of gift-giving and designed as a gift in itself, and booksellers ever since have designed special Christmas editions to make the most of it. In a similar tradition, I remember the various 'annuals' of my childhood, published each Christmas and centred round various sports or popular characters, which proliferate even today as stocking-filler staples.

Charles Dickens wrote three more Christmas stories which, if less well known today, were successful in their time, each selling out in many thousands in a matter of days. He captured the nostalgic mood of his time so much so that, on Christmas Day 1845, the *Morning Chronicle* newspaper wrote that he had been 'elected as chief literary master of the ceremonies for Christmas'.

His words passed into the vernacular. Over time, tradesmen came to permit their staff to take Bank Holidays off work rather than be called 'a Scrooge' or be accused of having a 'Bah Humbug' attitude. Christmas became a time for generosity, for practical benevolence and, where poverty pinched, it was felt that there was a public duty to alleviate it. It was an extraordinary achievement. Dickens nevertheless enjoyed himself and was always keen on Christmas parties. During this period, children took centre stage, whilst families set out to host the perfect Christmas dinner to celebrate the day properly.

Dickens died in June 1870, leaving his last novel, centred on the mystery of Edwin Drood's disappearance on Christmas Eve, unfinished. His funeral at Westminster Abbey was packed, although many of the mourners were also craning their necks to get a glimpse of another national treasure – Alfred, Lord Tennyson.

Tennyson also produced various poems about Christmas, as well as incorporating the festive season into his tales of chivalry and King Arthur, and it is hard to overestimate how famous he was at that time. His poems were instant bestsellers and he carried on the tradition of promoting the cosy family Christmas, looking askance at ribaldry and excess.

Tennyson was a central character and man of influence during the long reign of Queen Victoria, and the then Lord Carnarvon was thrilled to meet him twice at his home. However, a far more regular visitor to Highclere was a friend whose pen name was Lewis Carroll. His book, *Alice's Adventures in Wonderland*, full of fantastical creatures, was inscribed as 'A Christmas Gift to a Dear Child in Memory of a Summer Day'.

For all we have tamed so much of the world around us, there are still moments and places where a little fear lurks of an unexpected touch or a shadow we do not understand. Even at Highclere, when the gloaming light settles in around us, imagination can so easily take us all back to the darkness of the past and the ghost stories which proliferated in old rural parts of Britain.

LEFT
Snow settles on the espalier fig trees in the Monks' Garden

GHOST STORIES

A sad tale is best for winter: I have one
Of sprites and goblins
WILLIAM SHAKESPEARE, THE WINTER'S TALE

ONE WINTRY SUNDAY AFTERNOON, WHEN MY SON EDWARD
was only about three years old, Geordie, a photographer and I were alone
in the Castle taking photographs of the paintings in the Smoking Room
for a new guidebook I was writing. Inevitably, mid-afternoon, Edward
needed a change of scenery, so he and I set off through the green baize
door into the servery that sits behind the Dining Room, then down the
old servants' stairs into the basement. I had left his battery-powered, little
red ride-on car there for him and it was time to go and feed Percy, the
yellow Labrador puppy.

We headed through a set of doors, then made a right-hand turn along
the rather poorly lit corridor, followed by a second right-hand turn, then a
glance to my left showed me a man coming towards us out of the indistinct
gloom, dressed in dark clothes, with some sort of paler neck tie or cravat.
He was about my husband's height but seemed slightly undefined. I could
hear Percy barking madly, trapped a way off behind a further set of doors.

With Edward in front of me, his little feet carefully on the electric pedal, I urged greater speed. He, as usual, had his own ideas and his own pace. Glancing behind, the figure appeared to be following us so I began simply to push Edward along, 'Faster darling, put your foot down,' until we burst through the heavy swing doors to Percy, who was very loud and very anxious. The figure paused at the doors, and as we hurried along the last stretch of corridor, I did not look back.

Thereafter, I preferred to avoid this corridor conjunction, which made my progress around the Castle somewhat convoluted. This incident took place shortly after Geordie and I took over responsibility for Highclere, and after a while I thought I should resolve the situation. I asked Father Peter, an Anglican monk based at Westminster, if he would come down and bless the Castle.

Father Peter listened to my story and asked me to try to find out who the man might have been and what had happened. One story I found took place in the nineteenth century when a nursery nurse had been having a romance with a footman. While she was absent from the nursery, the Countess's baby had died. It was probably cot death or something similar, and nothing to do with the illicit couple, but in the pain, grief and misery thereafter the footman committed suicide not far from where I had seen the figure. He had lain down and slit his throat over a drain. I was again a new countess with a young child and perhaps he had hurried behind, anxious to see us safe.

House blessings often take place on the twelfth day of Christmas, which is Epiphany, 6 January. In my case I was unwilling to wait that long, and Father Peter undoubtedly had other duties to perform on that day, so he arrived one morning with prayers and holy water.

We spent a peaceful and thoughtful morning, beginning at the front door. Pausing in the Saloon, I realised, belatedly, that to go around all the rooms would surely mean we would run out of both holy water and time, but Father Peter was ahead of me and suggested we take a representative sample. Thus we went next into the Dining Room before going upstairs. I asked him to focus on the bedroom in which the 5th Earl of Carnarvon was rumoured to have held séances one hundred years previously. They were rather popular at that time and such interest in spiritualism and psychics was manifest in his contemporaries, from Arthur Conan Doyle to Carnarvon's friend Arthur Balfour, later Conservative Prime Minister.

From there, we went back downstairs into the much older part of the building and I stood nervously where the ghost had appeared and hoped this would work – that he would follow Father Peter's advice and we could wish him on his way. In the years since, I have not seen the figure again, so I presume the blessing worked. I do not think that area is necessarily wholly without ghosts, however, and when we have reconfigured various alarms and sensors along different passages, there are often a few false starts, with the fitters reporting feeling uncomfortable.

Pat Withers has worked at the Castle for over sixty years, joining her father as a painter and decorator. They were working near each other in the lower Castle corridor when her father saw a well-dressed lady in a floor-length black dress descend the Gothic stairs and walk past him before turning towards the kitchen. Politely he said, 'Good evening.' He didn't, however, hear his daughter Pat greet the lady so he went round to admonish her. Pat replied, 'No one came round here at all.'

Pat's best story for a winter's night was of one such a sighting when she had left two of her assistants, Richard and Darren, to close up the shutters. She had left to go down the Red Stairs to wash up the paint brushes when she looked up to see Darren, thoroughly spooked, hurtling down the stairs at a great pace before heading out of the Castle, across the courtyard and off down the road. He never did work in the Castle after that.

One particularly troublesome ghost at the end of the nineteenth century was banished to a 'yew tree' round the back of the Castle by a bevy of six visiting bishops and thence to the Red Sea (I am not sure why they chose that particular location) for one hundred years, or it might have been one hundred and fifty years. I am not sure, however, exactly on what date the term of banishment started and therefore when it might end, but I rather hope it was a symbolic term and thus forever. By description, he seemed to resemble the Green Man or Lord of Misrule and I would prefer him to remain mythical rather than join us as 'Ghost of the Present'.

We live in an old house with its inevitable creaks and groans, its stories and its inmates' imaginations. Nevertheless, today, it is, above all, a home, welcoming visitors, friends and family. The Gaelic blessing [left] sets out what it is to have a home.

THE GAELIC BLESSING

May you have -
Walls for the wind
And a roof for the rain,
And drinks beside the fire
Laughter to cheer you
And those you love near you,
And all that your
heart may desire

NATIVITY PLAYS

THE CELEBRATION OF BELIEF IN THE IMMACULATE
Conception of the Virgin Mary is celebrated through much of the Catholic world on 8 December, although the Eastern Christian Church first celebrated a 'Feast of the Conception of the Most Holy and All Pure Mother of God' on 9 December.

Whilst this is a public holiday in some parts of the world, sadly it is not in Britain. However, the telling of the birth of Jesus in the form of nativity plays is celebrated by children all over the world throughout the whole of December.

Some, like nursery school plays, are simple light occasions where you watch your three-year-old act out being the left leg of the donkey, while others are full-blown affairs in barns with real animals and possibly even a real baby. One girlfriend of mine rather considerately had her fourth child just in time for it to take centre stage in her third daughter's school nativity play, and I well remember the slight anxiety of the practice sessions that had to take place in order to teach the four-year-old playing Mary how to hold a newborn baby on stage.

In the Bible, the Christmas story is told through different narratives in both the gospels of Matthew and Luke. There undoubtedly was a great

ABOVE
The Nativity Scene at
Highclere Church

movement of people travelling to register for the Census decreed by Caesar Augustus, which led to Mary and Joseph travelling to Bethlehem. After the birth, Mary and Joseph sought refuge in Egypt to escape Herod's wrath, themselves becoming refugees.

Sadly, those seeking refuge and fleeing war, famine and natural disasters are a regular feature in our news today, and like many people, we at Highclere try to help. We do not set up a nativity scene at the Castle, instead we hold a special day over Christmas when we sing songs and play music to raise money for refugees – whether for medical relief or homelessness, specifically around the Middle East. Guests and visitors gather in the courtyard behind the Castle and, regardless of the weather, we raise our voices to remember those less fortunate than ourselves. Our musicians have at times played from within the stables and, whilst we have never been able to provide any oxen, there have on occasions been horses to give an earthy backdrop to our efforts.

Generations of my husband's family have helped the less fortunate on the Highclere Estate at this time of year, and an 1831 list of those felt to deserve help includes 'Eeles, Widow – bedridden 2 years, a blanket, rug or linen very acceptable', followed by 'Marshall – daughter to the Widow Eeles and keeps everything neat and clean – she has three children and would be very glad of a blanket'.

Particularly poignant is a reference to 'Nash – wife to one of the men transported – left with 5 children': John Nash was a top sawyer/carpenter, and one of five men taken to court after an incident at Burghclere, in Hampshire, as part of the Swing Riots of 1830, when labourers, driven to desperation by low wages, bad harvests and the loss of winter employment following the introduction of threshing machines, assembled to demand money or destroy machines.

A petition by the clergy and farmers of the parish described him as 'sober, honest and industrious' and suggested he had joined the riots against his will.

CAROL SERVICES

CAROLS HAVE BEEN NOTED SINCE THE FOURTH CENTURY AD, but they first appear in English about 1426 when a country chaplain, John Awdlay, listed twenty-five 'caroles of Cristemas', which were likely sung in the open air, just as ours are.

Alongside our efforts here, all the local churches near Highclere hold traditional carol services throughout December and my husband reads lessons at many of them. I am also sometimes asked to take part and on one memorable occasion, in order to raise money for two cancer charities, I had to assume a Yorkshire accent for the reading. I wrote it all out phonetically,

RIGHT
Frontispiece of a Bible
from the Highclere Library
dated 1701

THE
HOLY BIBLE,
CONTAINING THE
Old Testament and the New
Newly Translated out of the ORIGINAL TONGUES
And with the Former Translations diligently
Compared and Revised.
By His Majesties special Command.
APPOINTED to be read in CHURCHES

LONDON
Printed by CHARLES BILL and the Executrix of
THOMAS NEWCOMB deceas'd; Printers to
The Kings most Excellent Majestie.
CUM PRIVILEGIO.
M D CC I.

practising quite a few times and, although I say it myself, it was sufficiently close that various of the audience thought I was proper Yorkshire. *Downton Abbey* is supposedly set in Yorkshire, so it was all quite fitting for a service in Hampshire.

In the early- to mid-nineteenth century, few churches had organs, and carols would be accompanied by villagers playing instruments from violins to the serpent. A notebook used by the musicians at Hannington Church, a few miles from Highclere, in about 1830, is preserved in the Hampshire Record Office and includes the tunes of several Christmas carols.

We start to learn carols at nursery school and they follow us through our school years, through carol services we share with our parents and friends, so most of us still remember at least the first lines for all our lives. Many of them were written during Victorian times, although some may have earlier ancestry. St Francis of Assisi encouraged carols during worship and created a nativity scene in order to share the story.

Likewise, Martin Luther wrote carols, whilst music and song played a large part in Tudor Christmases. King Henry VIII dispensed hospitality in magnificent fashion, which he nevertheless married with solemn religious observances, attending mass first. A particular carol associated with this time, and one we still sing, is 'Tomorrow Shall Be My Dancing Day'.

Growing up in Cornwall, our carol services were more modest, but to my mind just as enchanting. The cliffs and headlands there are blessed with tiny

ABOVE
Dan's Lodge – one of the
follies on the Highclere Estate

ancient Norman chapels, with creaky organs and very little heating, a link to past congregations gathering out of the wintry weather to sing together.

Our mother, who had a lovely voice, would inevitably sing every descant, usually as a solo, and we would stand in the pews beside her, carrying on as normal, feeling childish embarrassment. I can still hear her voice in my head and I smile at the memories, which have now become treasured. Equally, she always enjoyed listening to the Festival of Nine Lessons and Carols that is held in King's College Chapel, in Cambridge, at 3pm on Christmas Eve. First introduced in 1918, it is now broadcast on the radio to millions of people around the world and it has become a tradition to stop and enjoy it, as a marker on the journey to Christmas Day.

SAINT LUCY'S DAY

ACCORDING TO LEGEND, ST LUCY WAS A THIRD-CENTURY martyr who brought food and aid to Christians hiding in the Roman catacombs by wearing a candle-lit wreath to light her way, thus leaving her hands free to carry as much food as possible. She was blinded for her faith and since her saint's day, 13 December, was at one point, before the calendar reforms, the shortest day of the year, this feast day became a Christian festival of light.

In Scandinavia she is represented as a lady wearing a white dress with a red sash. Songs are sung and girls dressed as St Lucy give out cookies and saffron buns. Norwegians call it Lussinatten, the longest night of the year, when no work was to be done unless they wished to be punished by Lussi, the fearsome enchantress.

Highclere Church does not hold a service for St Lucy but it does hold a Christingle service. This includes prayers, readings, hymns and carols and the lighting of the Christingle, a candle that represents God as the light of the world embedded in an orange, which symbolises the world, and wrapped in a red ribbon that represents Christ's blood. Rather like the St Lucy Day celebrations, it again puts children at the centre of Christmas.

WASSAILING

EARLY IN DECEMBER THE ESTATE OFFICE TEAM, AIDED and abetted by Pat and Mike Withers, who have lived and worked at Highclere forever and who are stalwart supporters, declare that they are off to the Wassail in Highclere Village Hall. The evening includes singing, traditionally without any musical instruments, drinking and possibly sharing the wassail cup.

The word 'wassail' comes from the Anglo-Saxon greeting 'Wæs þu hæl', meaning 'be thou hale', thus wishing each other good health.

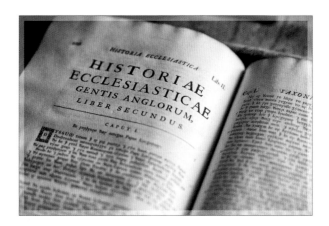

Recipes for a modern
WASSAIL CUP
PAGE 134
which is perfect to
accompany some
HIGHCLERE
MINCE PIES
PAGE 90

Highclere's Library boasts a rather beautiful, large, eighteenth-century bound book of Bede's *Ecclesiastical History of England*. Originally written in the ninth century during the reign of Alfred the Great, in both Latin and Anglo-Saxon, it is a key historical reference source for the Anglo-Saxon period.

Three hundred years after Bede, Geoffrey of Monmouth wrote *The History of the Kings of Britain*, claiming definitive authority, if speculative sources. His story was that King Vortigern shared a feast with a German prince where a beautiful girl offered the King a golden goblet full of wine and drunk his health saying 'Laverd king was hail'.

The traditional 'wassail' cup is made from warmed ale, cloves, nutmeg, sugar, eggs and roasted apples and this drink was quickly adopted into the custom of visiting your neighbours with the wassail cup, singing carols as you went. In some counties of England the wassailers would also go into the orchard to bless the apple trees, perhaps drink some cider and frighten away any evil spirits.

In return for the singing, householders would offer the wassailers some figgy pudding – hence the carol 'We Wish you a Merry Christmas', which includes the line 'Bring us some figgy pudding ... We won't go until we get some, so bring some out here!' Once the carols were sung, the residents would give them money, hot mince pies and perhaps some tangerines.

Strictly speaking, wassailing should take place in January, which might be a welcome interruption from the stoic idea of a dry January and a fine time to think about spring and apple blossom.

Pat Withers and our wassailing posse stay warm in the village hall; they do not need to stamp their feet in the muffled snow or blow on their fingers to keep warm, and while there is a raffle to raise money for charity, they don't get paid for their singing!

THE HIGHCLERE CHRISTMAS QUIZ

PART 3

ART & ARCHITECTURE

1/ Architect Sir Charles Barry remodelled the Castle in the mid-1800s. Which famous London palace did he design?

2/ The Bishops of Winchester had a palace at Highclere from the 13th century, but which notable Bishop and architect carried out extensive work in the late 14th century?

3/ William of Wykeham was a founder of two educational institutions and used oak trees from Highclere to aid their construction. Can you name either or both?

4/ Siddown Hill is the third highest hill in Hampshire, but what is the name of the folly that sits on it in the Highclere Estate?

5/ A large portrait of Charles I hangs in the dining room of both Downton Abbey and Highclere. To whom is the portrait attributed?

6/ Another of the three follies in the Castle grounds and estate is the Temple of Diana. What was Diana the Roman goddess of?

7/ Capability Brown drew up plans to redesign the grounds in the 1770s, but what was Capability's real name?

8/ Coade stone was used in the construction of London Lodge, and was produced in the 1770s by Mrs Coade's Artificial Stone Company. Mrs Coade shared a first name with her daughter who took over the business. What was that first name, and why was the second Mrs Coade unusual?

9/ There are a number of pieces of Meissen porcelain in the drawing room at Highclere. What was the signature trademark that Meissen introduced in 1720 to protect its production?

WHO SAID...

10/ Disraeli was a house guest at Highclere, and was Prime Minister twice during his lifetime. He is also famous for saying; 'There are three kinds of lies' …
How did he continue?

HIGHCLERE TODAY

11/ How long is the drive from the Castle gate to the front door?

ANSWERS

10/ 'There are three kinds of lies; lies, damn lies and statistics' 11/ 1½ miles
7/ Lancelot 8/ Eleanor, and the second Mrs Coade never married (Mrs. was a courtesy title) 9/ Crossed swords
New College, Oxford 4/ Heaven's Gate 5/ Sir Anthony Van Dyck 6/ Goddess of the hunt, moon and nature
1/ The Houses of Parliament/Palace of Westminster 2/ Bishop William of Wykeham 3/ Winchester College;

1860s SCONE/CAKE

We have tried making this recipe from the Castle archives and when it came out of the oven it was lovely and warm, so naturally we had to taste it immediately ... and continued tasting as we could not decide whether it was more like a scone or a cake. Try it and see what you think!

PREPARATION TIME **15 mins** COOKING TIME **25 mins** SERVES **6–8**

INGREDIENTS

225g (8oz) self-raising flour, plus extra for dusting
1 tsp baking powder (invented in 1855 and so used by the 4th Countess's chefs)
½ tsp salt
50g (2oz) cold butter (straight from the fridge), diced
30g (1¼oz) caster sugar
125ml (4fl oz) milk
1 egg, beaten
Jam and clotted cream, to serve

METHOD

§   Preheat the oven to 210°C/410°F/Gas mark 6.

§   Sift the flour, baking powder and salt into a mixing bowl.

§   Add the butter and use your fingertips to mix it in with the flour and baking powder until it is like fine breadcrumbs.

§   Stir in the sugar.

§   Add the milk and egg to a measuring jug and whisk together.

§   Carefully add just enough of the milk mix to the flour until it becomes a soft dough, keeping a little of the mixture for later.

§   Turn out the dough onto a floured worktop and quickly shape into a simple round (or a ring shape if you are feeling ambitious) about 2cm (¾ inch) thick.

§   Put onto a floured baking tray and brush lightly with the reserved milk/egg mixture.

§   Bake in the hot oven for 20–25 minutes until brown and well risen. It should also sound hollow when tapped on the bottom.

§   Put a clean tea towel on a wire rack. Carefully lift the scone off the baking sheet with a palette knife onto the tea towel and wrap it around the scone.

§   Slice the scone in half and fill with your favourite jam and clotted cream before serving.

[CHEF'S TIP: The mixture can be made in advance and kept in a container in the fridge. The secret to good scones is that the butter and milk used must be cold, you should handle the dough as little as possible, and wrap the cooked scone in a tea towel while cooling.]

§   If you like, dried fruit such as sultanas or cranberries can be added to the dough just before adding the milk.

PHEASANT WITH MADEIRA

Pheasant is plentiful and inexpensive during the shooting season (between 1 October and 1 February in Britain) and it makes a welcome change from turkey at Christmas.

PREPARATION TIME **15 mins** COOKING TIME **40 mins** SERVES **4**

INGREDIENTS

60g (2½oz) butter

2 tbsp olive oil

2 oven-ready pheasants, jointed into breasts and legs (with thighs)

4 rashers smoked back bacon (or slices of Parma ham)

4 banana shallots, finely diced

2 celery stalks, finely diced

1 carrot, peeled and finely diced

½ leek (white part only), washed and finely chopped

2 star anise

250ml (9fl oz) Madeira

200ml (7fl oz) game or chicken stock (shop purchased is fine)

Salt and pepper

METHOD

§   Preheat the oven to 180°C/350°F/Gas mark 4.

§   Heat the butter and oil in a casserole dish over a medium–high heat. Season the pheasants with a little salt and pepper, then add the pheasant legs to the pan. Gently brown them on all sides until completely sealed, then remove.

§   In the same dish, seal the skin side only of the pheasant breast. When golden brown, remove from the pan and keep with the legs. When cool enough to handle, carefully wrap a rasher of bacon (or you can use Parma ham for more decadence) around each breast.

§   To the same casserole dish, add the shallots, celery, carrot, leek and star anise with a little more butter, if needed, and cook until all the vegetables are soft. Return the legs to the pan and cover with the Madeira and stock. Put a lid on the pan and place the casserole into the oven for 15 minutes.

§   Remove the pan and add the breasts, skin side up, to the hot stock and return to the oven for a further 10 minutes with the lid off.

§   Remove all the meat from the pan and keep to one side. Strain the vegetables from the stock and discard. Return the stock to the pan and place on the hob over a high heat until it is reduced by half – this will give you a nice jus.

§   Serve a carved breast alongside a braised leg per person, along with some jus.

MULLED WINE

This is a great, easy recipe for a lovely festive, warming drink. The aroma of it is the very essence of Christmas. For children and those who prefer to avoid alcohol, I have also included a mulled apple juice recipe here, which is very popular with our stallholders at the Christmas Fair.

INGREDIENTS

1 bottle of good red wine
250ml (9fl oz)
    fresh orange juice
250ml (9fl oz)
    blood orange purée
100g (3½oz)
    muscovado sugar
2 bay leaves
2 cloves
1 star anise
Seeds of 1 vanilla pod
1 cinnamon stick
2 red chillies

METHOD

§   Place all the ingredients into a heavy-based pan and over a low heat bring up to a temperature of 72°C (162°F) to dissolve the sugar (use a sugar thermometer for accuracy).

§   Pour into a serving bowl and allow to cool, then drink at a comfortable temperature of 60°C (140°F).

MULLED APPLE JUICE

INGREDIENTS

1 litre (1¾ pints) fresh
    apple juice
6 strips of orange peel
1 cinnamon stick
3 cloves
Honey, to taste

METHOD

§   Mix the apple juice with the strips of orange peel, cinnamon stick and cloves and simmer for about 10 minutes until all the flavours have infused.

§   Sweeten with honey to taste.

WASSAIL CUP

INGREDIENTS

1·5 litres (2½ pints) of
    either ale, or half ale and
    half stout, or cider
250g (9oz) demerara sugar
1 tsp each of cloves,
    cinnamon, allspice and
    grated nutmeg
300ml (10½fl oz) sherry
Peel of 1 lemon and 2 or 3
    slices of the same lemon
6–7 apples, cored

METHOD

§   Bake the apples in a medium oven for 20 minutes, remove and leave to one side.

§   Warm a large bowl by filling with hot water and leave to one side.

§   Bring half the ale (or other choice) plus the sugar and spices to the boil in a large saucepan. Stir until the sugar is dissolved, then take off the heat.

§   Add the remaining ale and the sherry. Empty the water out of the wassail bowl and pour in the contents of the saucepan.

§   Add 3 to 4 lemon slices and the baked apples. Scrunch the lemon peel over the bowl.

HIGHCLERE CASTLE MULLED WINE PUDDING

This is an excellent way to use up leftover mulled wine and equally to make a different bread pudding, which you can prepare ahead. It has lovely dark Christmas colours, and when decorated with a few cinnamon sticks, mint leaves and berries it looks spectacular.

PREPARATION TIME 20 mins, plus chilling overnight   COOKING TIME 5 mins   SERVES 6

INGREDIENTS

1 bottle of good red wine
2 cinnamon sticks,
    plus extra to decorate
Grated nutmeg, to taste
1 vanilla pod, split
4 cloves
2 star anise, plus extra
    to decorate
Zest and juice
    of 1 blood orange
200g (7oz) redcurrant jelly
150g (5oz) sugar (to taste)
4 leaves of gelatine (or agar
    agar for vegetarians)
750g (1lb 10½oz) winter
    fruit and berries mix
    (apples, pears, blood
    oranges, cranberries,
    passion fruit, quince;
    don't be afraid to
    use frozen berries
    like raspberries and
    redcurrants), plus 150g
    (5oz) to decorate
1 loaf day-old white sliced
    bread, crusts removed
10 mint leaves, to decorate
Clotted cream, to serve

METHOD

§   Pour the red wine into a large heavy-based pan and add the cinnamon sticks, nutmeg, vanilla pod, cloves, star anise, the zest and juice of the blood orange and the redcurrant jelly. Bring to the boil.

§   When hot, add sugar to taste and reduce the liquid by half. This will give you a wonderful cooking stock in which to soak the fruit and bread for your pudding.

§   Soak the gelatine in a little water until soft.

§   Slice larger fruit into bite-size pieces, then add all the fruit to the red wine reduction and gently simmer for no more than 5 minutes to soften. Add the gelatine and dissolve, being careful not to crush the fruit.

§   Taste and correct the sweetness if necessary. Strain out the fruit and put it to one side, keeping all the warm mulled wine stock.

§   Dip the bread into the mulled wine stock and line the inside of a 1·5 litre (2½ pint) pudding bowl with the ruby red slices.

§   When fully lined, spoon in the fruit. Feel free to add a layer of bread to the middle of the pudding, if you so desire, for extra support. Pour in most of the remaining wine stock, but save some to pour over the finished pudding when you turn it out the next day.

§   Cover the base with more bread slices. You can press the pudding to help maintain its shape, using a small weight (a tin of beans is ideal) on an upturned plate. Chill the pudding in the fridge overnight.

§   When ready to serve, turn the pudding out onto a plate and pour over the remaining wine stock (if this has set, just warm it slightly to bring it back to pouring consistency).

§   Garnish with berries, cinnamon sticks, star anise, some mint leaves and serve with the clotted cream.

ORANGES IN COINTREAU

Food can be extraordinarily evocative, and this particular dish brings back memories of my mother making it. Food is about sight, taste and smell but this simple pudding, which you can prepare ahead, just reminds me of my childhood and our wonderful mother. The colour is perfect for wintry evenings and you can serve it with thick Greek yoghurt.

PREPARATION TIME 20 mins, plus cooling and chilling   COOKING TIME 10 mins   SERVES 4

INGREDIENTS

8 small oranges
100g (3½oz) caster sugar
4 tbsp water
4 tbsp Cointreau

METHOD

§   Remove the zest from the oranges, then cut it into shreds.

§   Put the sugar and water in a large heavy-based saucepan and stir over a very low heat until the sugar has dissolved, then bring to the boil.

§   Add the orange shreds and boil for 1 minute, then remove them with a slotted spoon and pat them dry on a piece of kitchen paper. Set aside and leave the syrup to cool.

§   Peel the oranges with a sharp knife, removing every scrap of white pith and taking care not to damage the orange flesh.

§   Cut the oranges across into thin slices and transfer to a serving dish.

§   Add the Cointreau to the cooled syrup, then pour this over the oranges. Refrigerate for at least 1 hour, spooning the juice over the oranges from time to time.

§   To serve, sprinkle the oranges with the zest and serve at once, perhaps with some thickly whipped cream.

CHAPTER EIGHT

ENTERTAINING

❦ WHETHER A HOME IS ❦

LARGE OR SMALL, ENTERTAINING IS ABOUT

BRINGING PEOPLE TOGETHER WITH DELICIOUS
drinks and delectable food. Sometimes a theme helps, too. Pericles,
who built many of the monuments in Athens, said: 'What you
leave behind is not what is engraved in stone monuments, but
what is woven into the lives of others.' He may have had more
serious thoughts behind his comments, yet spending time together
over drinks or dinner makes us all feel welcome and valued.

THROUGHOUT HISTORY, MIDWINTER ENTERTAINING
was always a highlight of this season. From kings and their courts to
squires and their agents, all were more popular if they offered celebrations
and entertainment. It was a time to gather together and share hospitality.
Nowadays this occasion can be a meal, a formal dinner, a party or gala – it
doesn't really matter.

Apart from occasionally studying at St Andrews University, myself and my
flatmate Smiles (her real name is Susannah) organised a number of parties
during our time there. We had a vodka party (every course of food had a
vodka base), as well as evenings themed with 'Gin and Sin' and 'Raincoats and
Dark Glasses'. Most were self-explanatory, and I learnt an enormous number
of cooking tips from Smiles, who was very adept and good at planning.

COCKTAIL PARTIES

NOËL COWARD REMARKED, 'IT'S NEVER TOO EARLY FOR
a cocktail' – and he's right, they do lend a frisson of glamour and thrill to
an evening. There is some dispute as to the origin of the cocktail; some
say it originated in New Orleans, others claim it was invented in the bar at

The Savoy, in London. At any event, by the 1860s they had become popular on both sides of the Atlantic. Oddly enough, the name is derived from horses. In the eighteenth century it was customary to dock the tails of horses that were not thoroughbred, and these were called cocktailed horses or, simply, cocktails. Therefore, by extension, the word cocktail was applied to an alcoholic drink that had been diluted, which was not a 'purebred' drink.

The 6th Earl of Carnarvon met Noël Coward and certainly enjoyed the world of plays and musicals, delighting in the company of amusing women from the world of the stage. A favourite cocktail at Highclere during the 1930s was a White Lady, which given the cold glass and egg whites has a suitably ghostly appearance.

Several establishments take the credit for originating the White Lady, including the famous bartender Harry MacElhone while he was working at Ciro's Club, in London, in 1919, or at his own Harry's New York Bar, in Paris. The recipe was included in *The Savoy Cocktail Book* in 1930, and apparently White Lady was one of Laurel and Hardy's favourite drinks.

Alec Waugh, the novelist and elder brother of Evelyn Waugh, claimed he first invented the cocktail party in London in 1925. He said: 'There was nothing to do on winter evenings between half-past five and half-past seven.' These occasions were, from the outset, considered scandalous, immoral and, without doubt, decadent.

Evelyn Waugh, who was, incidentally, married to firstly Evelyn and then to Laura – both nieces of the 5th Earl of Carnarvon – incorporated a cocktail party into many of his novels, also involving a denouement of some sort.

F. Scott Fitzgerald described a summer party stocked with cocktails in his 1925 novel *The Great Gatsby*:

Recipe for a classic
Highclere cocktail:
WHITE LADY
PAGE 111

There was music from my neighbour's house through the summer nights. In his blue gardens men and girls came and went like moths among the whisperings and the champagne and the stars... In the main hall a bar with a real brass rail was set up, and stocked with gins and liquors and with cordials...

WE DO STILL HOST COCKTAIL PARTIES HERE AT
Highclere, but with a different flavour from those of nearly one hundred
years ago – not just because it is a very different time of year (we hold
them mainly at Christmas) but also because they are often given to raise
money for a particular charity. If guests used to arrive a fashionable twenty
minutes late in the 1920s, today, given the journey from London, they are
often on time or even early. With music and a theme, it is an evening of
laughter and new friends as well as old.

Each December we support a different charity. Last year, we hosted a
Christmas Champagne evening to celebrate the one-hundredth anniversary
of the Royal Air Force. It was a punctuation mark at the end of a busy year
of fundraising for them. We were joined by the Chief of the Air Staff along
with a number of RAF personnel and their wives or partners. The theme
was magic and carols and the magician brought surprised delight before
the carols marked the end of the evening.

The wonderful women of the Military Wives choir lined up along the
Oak Staircase as we all thronged around the Christmas tree in the Saloon.
This choir is comprised of wives, partners and widows of British Military
personnel, as well as servicewomen and veterans. Formed in 2010, the choir
has performed at major military events and also at the Queen's Diamond
Jubilee Concert. The collected pilots decided to cluster together and lead
the singing, which caused great hilarity and goodwill, as well as some
interesting verses!

Earlier in the year we had hosted a charity weekend called 'Heroes at
Highclere – for those who serve and those who save'. The exhibition from
that event, which told the stories of the eight aircraft and their crews who

crashed on the Estate during the Second World War, was on display in the Library and Music Room for the party, and those brave men were very much on our minds. The current men, serving today, sang for their forbears and absent friends as well as for all of our amusement. 'Jingle Bells' went particularly well at the very end.

PLANNING YOUR COCKTAIL PARTY

Highclere is a marvellous setting for a cocktail party, but growing up in Cornwall at Christmas, in a large windblown house above a beach, we had just as much fun asking friends over for more casual drinks, proving it does not need to cost the earth to host a successful event.

The beauty of a cocktail party is that it is not the commitment of a 5-6-hour dinner party and everyone can talk to who they want. The trick to a successful evening is to keep it simple.

Plan ahead. Prepare as much of the food as you can and get drinks ready and chilled. Make sure you have the right glasses and serving plates, plus napkins, so your guests don't get sticky fingers, and make sure you have enough ice.

Remember, spirits go further than wine, but avoid rich and creamy cocktails as they don't work well with canapés. Serve one alcoholic cocktail and a soft drink. We usually offer sparkling elderflower.

Offer delectable bites to eat, but nothing too big. Everything should be able to be eaten in one mouthful.

Assume 20 per cent of your guests won't come, but cater for 100 per cent and allow three drinks per guest per hour.

Work out the number of guests you can fit into your space. Roughly speaking, divide the square footage of the room by five as each person needs 1·5m/5 foot of personal space.

Give your guests clear guidelines as to the dress code, so that everyone feels comfortable.

Set the mood with lighting, flowers, candles and music.

The average party length is 2-3 hours, most popularly from 7-9pm, so space out the food and drink through the evening.

Have a trusted sidekick to help get the party going. Introduce your guests to each other. Remember, cocktail parties should be full of chatter and laughter.

DINNER PARTIES

I HAVE VARIOUS FAVOURITE DINNER-PARTY SCENES FROM films. One is from a later scene in *Bridget Jones's Diary*, where four hours of cooking a celebratory dinner culminated in blue-string soup and marmalade. However, as Maya Angelou wisely said, 'People will forget what you did but they will never forget how you made them feel', and that is definitely my view on entertaining.

Once again, the secret to a dinner party that you enjoy as much as your guests is to plan, plan, plan. Settle on a style, then assess the budget and the occasion. Plan what drinks you will offer. When you choose a menu, work out how you are going to serve it, too. Remember, it is a time for celebration and entertaining and should not be stressful, so use proven recipes. It is helpful to prepare the first course and the pudding the day before so that they are ready to go, then all you need to do is focus on the main course.

A beautifully decorated table is a frame for the food you are serving. Select a colour palette that complements your home and arrange the flowers the evening before. Use variations in height in order to add perspective, but don't make it so high that people can't see over it. The trick is to complement rather than overwhelm, so don't choose flowers that are too highly perfumed and, of course, no scented candles on the dinner table.

ABOVE
Lady Carnarvon adds the placement cards to the table

Welcoming guests is all about hospitality and indulgence, so do not run out of food; if you are worried, prepare a cheeseboard to cover up any shortages. Ultimately, enjoy yourself – relax and spend time with your guests: memories are made with people and through conversations. Afterwards, love your leftovers – they can become soups or supper on another day.

DINNER PARTIES IN THE DINING ROOM AT HIGHCLERE are organised on a larger scale but we hope that they are still entertaining and memorable for all our guests. Paul, our chef, asks me what I would like, whether he can experiment and what flavour, in every sense, I am looking for. Following his thoughtful suggestions, I look through the menu and see what Geordie thinks. Once it is agreed, Geordie will consult Luis about the choice of wines whilst I tend to ask Luis for a choice of his specials (cocktails) and, if I can, set out the placement cards well ahead of time.

Luis's team take the afternoon to set the table and prepare the individual stamped butter dishes placed in front of each guest. Then they give a last polish to the silver whilst I finish the flowers.

In case the cocktails don't quite succeed in breaking the ice in the first part of the evening, I sometimes write our guests' place names in hieroglyphs for further amusement. It does take rather a long time, though, and I tend to regret the decision before I am even halfway through. Alternatively, I make up riddles and clues around their names or jobs. Thus finding everyone's place takes time, but it is entertaining and everyone then has to read out their riddle later on in the dinner.

Highclere is large, grand and stately, yet it is a home, too, and planning some sort of after-dinner amusements continues the feeling of magic and fun of an evening.

K A R A O K E !

GROWING UP, YOU ALWAYS THINK YOU WILL NOT BE LIKE your parents; that you will do things differently and not the annoying way they did them. In reality, I find I often do just as they did, and thus in turn really annoy or embarrass my son.

One of the best evenings we had here was when I had hired a karaoke machine for Geordie's birthday dinner. It was duly plugged in and set up in the Library for after-dinner amusement. My mother-in-law was ensconced on the sofa by the fire with a little coffee and selection of petits fours.

The first song was selected and the first backward-coming contributors were encouraged. To begin with it was rather hit and miss, before our New York friends, Annie and Steven, took over and gave a great rendition of 'New York, New York' – dance steps included. Some of the songs and singing were truly interesting and I glanced at my girlfriend, Rona, to see

tears streaming down her face as she was laughing so much. About six men were standing round the machine and really making some noise – it was a wonderful sight.

No one *had* to take part, and whilst it might not have been the 'coolest' evening, my memories of it are of laughter and fun. Maybe we should repeat it soon ...

THE STEINWAY PIANO

WITHIN THE RICHLY DECORATED, GREEN, FRENCH-SILK walls of the Drawing Room stands our Steinway piano, a beautiful instrument, originally made in Hamburg and shipped to London in January 1890, before it made its way to Highclere. It was bought by Almina, who, as the new wife of the 5th Earl, set about furnishing and decorating the Castle in style, subsidised by her father, Alfred de Rothschild. His generosity enabled her to refurbish the house and throw lavish parties, with every need catered for, for guests that included the Prince of Wales.

It never ceases to amaze me that, when sitting down at the piano here, my fingers run over keys that have likely been touched by rather more adept

musicians than myself. Over the years it has been played by noted Victorian pianists, in the 1930s by Sir Malcolm Sargent, and by recent composers such as John Lunn, who wrote the music for *Downton Abbey*.

Extraordinary singers such as Morgan Pearse have sung beside it, too – a rare privilege. When the renowned soprano Dame Kiri Te Kanawa appeared in an episode of *Downton Abbey*, we were enthralled to hear her warm up behind the scenes, and time seemed to stand still on hearing her richly effortless voice resonate around the Saloon and ground-floor rooms.

We always welcome guests who can 'do a turn', and we have often been entertained with singing – both classical and modern. Apart from the more public performances, though, it also brings much family pleasure. My number-five sister, Penny, is a lovely pianist and, one December, she brought down some popular song music to play one evening after supper. As a mother of small children, however, she was tired and so disappeared to bed after supper, leaving just her music.

We had all been looking forward to it, so two of Geordie's friends from his Oxford University days stepped in and offered to play. Unfamiliar with the music, they said they would have to take it slowly. Some of the assembled guests had very nice voices and stood grouped around the piano with the sheets of words I had prepared.

Led by my husband, they started off with the theme tune from *Titanic*. Unfortunately, the speed of play was such that ten minutes later they were all manfully still singing about going on and on and on. I was howling with laughter, utterly unable to speak and certainly not able to sing about going on. I suspect that earlier pianists may have been more accomplished and the audience more decorous but we really did enjoy it, it was a proper team effort.

At Christmas, the piano has a less glamorous role, though, being firstly used as a stand for a stallholder selling handmade crackers during the Christmas fair and then to display many of our Christmas cards.

OFFICE PARTIES
& STAFF DANCING

DURING THE YEAR THERE ARE VARIOUS STAFF EVENTS that they plan themselves: a rounders' match, theatre trip or the wonderful Guides' Christmas drinks organised by head guide Diana. There is also always an official Farm Christmas dinner and a Castle Christmas dinner in one or other of the local pubs.

Well in advance, I had booked a pub for the Castle one, the date was in the diary, then Julia from the Castle office took charge with verve. On the appointed evening in December, thirty or forty of us gathered in Kingsclere and were all given Christmas hats to wear.

Once underway, Julia took centre stage handing out quiz sheets for each of the four tables. Encouraging us, leading us astray, Julia's quiz occupied us with much hilarity. Luis was always trying to cheat and look up things on his phone, whilst my husband thought he would go off-piste and make up ditties and rhymes to sing, which he found very funny (as did we).

The dinner that night was excellent and marked the end of many of the events for the public before we turned to gather as families in our respective homes.

IN THE NINETEENTH CENTURY, RATHER THAN THE office parties of today, there was always a Servants' Ball just after Christmas. The Library was cleared, the smooth polished-oak floor gleamed but was not too slippery – although if anyone did fall down, it led to a roar of laughter. There were two sets, including, at various times, a waltz, quadrille, gallop, schottische, mazurka and polka variations.

There was also an excellent supper laid out in the servants' dining room, and a wonderful time was had by all.

If balls with other local houses and their staff were planned there was often spontaneous dancing, as a maid's diary recalls:

25 December, Thursday 1884
Highclere

Very cold — but a very pleasant and happy Christmas Day. In the evening the children, with a good many of the maids, danced in the drawing room whilst Elsie played on the piano — and I danced with Mervyn till I was so tired I could go on no longer.

So ends 1884 — a stormy political year — of g[rea]t anxiety — much work closing in remarkable quiet — Personally what have I not to be thankful for — wife, children all well and doing well.

THE HIGHCLERE CHRISTMAS QUIZ

PART 4

P E O P L E

1/ Stanhope bedroom was redecorated by the 5th countess of Carnarvon, Almina, in preparation for an eminent visitor. Who was that visitor?

2/ What is the name of *Downton Abbey*'s Cora/Lady Grantham's mother, and the name of the actress who played her?

3/ Almina was married to the 5th Earl, but who was her father?

4/ Geoffrey de Havilland made his first flight from Highclere, but can you name either of his two famous actress cousins?

5/ Matthew Crawley is named as heir to Downton Abbey, but how is he related to the Earl of Grantham?

6/ The current Earl of Carnarvon and the Earl of Grantham are which generation of Earls respectively?

7/ What is the name of the Earl of Grantham's original valet before he was replaced by Mr Bates?

8/ Dame Maggie Smith plays the Dowager Countess in *Downton Abbey*, but can you name one other titled Lady (of many) that she has played on film and the film title?

9/ Which Earl of Carnarvon discovered the tomb of Tutankhamun?

10/ Which character in *Downton Abbey* died of Spanish flu, and why was her death convenient?

11/ Stanhope bedroom was the scene of an infamous tryst between Lady Mary and Mr Pamuk, but what country was Mr Pamuk from, and what was his job?

WHO SAID...

12/ 'Of course I'll marry you, you old booby. I thought you'd never ask.' ... and to whom?

HIGHCLERE TODAY

13/ Who narrates the Highclere Castle app?

ANSWERS

12/ Mrs Hughes to Mr Carson 13/ Jim Carter (aka Carson)
She was engaged to Matthew Crawley, who was now free to marry Lady Mary 11/ Turkey – he was a diplomat
Lady Myra Naylor in *The Last September*; Lady Hester Random in *Tea With Mussolini*;
Grantham: 7th 7/ Mr Watson 8/ Lady Isabel Ames in *The Missionary*; Lady Hester Random in *Tea With Mussolini*; 9/ The 5th Earl 10/ Lavinia Swire.
4/ Olivia de Havilland; Joan Fontaine 5/ He is Robert's third cousin once removed 6/ Carnarvon: 8th;
1/ The Prince of Wales (the future George V) 2/ Martha Levinson; Shirley MacLaine 3/ Alfred de Rothschild

153

CANAPÉS

Canapés should be delicious and small enough to eat in one mouthful. The following are popular with most guests and look tempting on colourful platters.

HONEY, MUSTARD, SOY AND SESAME CHICKEN

PREPARATION TIME 15 mins, plus 1 hour marinating COOKING TIME 12–15 mins SERVES 6

INGREDIENTS

60g (2½oz) runny honey
1 tbsp wholegrain mustard
60ml (2½fl oz)
    light soy sauce
200g (7oz) skinless chicken
    breast, cut into slivers
1 tbsp sesame seeds, toasted
    (optional)

METHOD

§　Place the honey, mustard and soy sauce into a bowl and mix well.

§　Add the strips of chicken to the sauce and mix well to ensure they are all well coated in the marinade.

§　Cover and leave in the fridge to marinate for at least 1 hour.

§　Soak some bamboo skewers in a little cold water to help stop them burning in the oven (or use metal ones), then thread the chicken pieces onto the sticks.

§　Line a baking tray with greaseproof paper, arrange the chicken skewers on the tray and bake in the centre of the oven for 12–15 minutes, checking the chicken is cooked through and the juices are running clear.

§　Sprinkle with toasted sesame seeds, if you like, then serve immediately.

GARLIC PRAWN SKEWERS

PREPARATION TIME 10 mins, plus marinating COOKING TIME 5 mins SERVES 6

INGREDIENTS

1 bulb garlic, peeled
50ml (2fl oz) vegetable oil
200g (7oz) shelled,
    deveined raw tiger or
    king prawns
Knob of butter, for frying
Salt and pepper

METHOD

§　Blitz the garlic in a bowl using a hand-held blender, slowly adding the oil to form a paste.

§　Coat the prawns in this paste and leave to marinate for at least 20 minutes, longer if you like a more pronounced flavour.

§　Soak some bamboo skewers in a little cold water to help stop them burning in the pan (or use metal ones), then thread the prawns in twos or threes onto them.

§　When ready to serve, heat a frying pan over a medium heat and add the butter.

§　As the butter starts to foam, add the prawns in batches, depending on what you can fit into your pan.

§　Lightly fry for 1–2 minutes on each side, season with salt and pepper to taste, and serve immediately.

WILD MUSHROOM ARANCINI

These are scrumptious and most of the preparation can be done ahead of time.

PREPARATION TIME **20 mins**   COOKING TIME **2 hrs 15 mins, plus cooling**   MAKES **around 40**

INGREDIENTS

20g (¾oz) unsalted butter
300g (10½oz) mixed
    wild mushrooms,
    roughly chopped
1 large onion, diced
2 garlic cloves, crushed
400g (14oz) good risotto
    rice (we use Arborio)
1 bay leaf
2 litres (3½ pints)
    hot vegetable stock
150ml (5fl oz) Madeira
100g (3½oz) Parmesan
A sprig of thyme,
    some chervil and chives,
    chopped
50g (2oz) plain flour
1 egg, beaten
100g (3½oz) breadcrumbs
Vegetable oil, for frying
Salt and pepper

METHOD

§   Heat the butter in a large saucepan or casserole dish, add the wild mushrooms and cook for 10 minutes or so until just cooked. Remove the mushrooms with a slotted spoon, leaving any butter in the pan.

§   Add the onion and sweat down for 5–6 minutes. Add the crushed garlic and cook for another minute, adding more butter if needed. Now add the rice to the pan with the bay leaf, and pour in the hot stock a little bit at a time, stirring continuously.

§   Cook the rice until it is al dente, using as much stock as needed.

§   Add the Madeira and cook until the liquid has evaporated. Remove from the heat.

§   Stir in the grated Parmesan along with the chopped herbs. Then return the wild mushrooms to the pan with some seasoning and mix well.

§   Transfer the risotto to a container and leave to cool before refrigerating. (You can make this the day before and refrigerate overnight if you want to get ahead.)

§   When cold, the risotto should be firm enough for you to roll into small golf-ball-sized rounds – the arancini.

§   Set out three dishes: one with the flour, one with the egg and one with the breadcrumbs. Roll your arancini in the flour, to get a light and even coating, then dip into the egg and finally the breadcrumbs. You may wish to repeat the egg and breadcrumb stages if you like your breading thicker.

§   When all the arancini are prepared, half-fill a large pan with vegetable oil and heat to 180°C (350°F) – use a cook's thermometer for accuracy.

§   Fry the arancini, in batches, for 5–6 minutes, until golden brown and delicious. Drain on kitchen paper, sprinkle with a little salt and serve immediately.

CHEESE PUFFS

These delightful savoury bites are perfect for a cocktail party.

PREPARATION TIME **20 mins** COOKING TIME **30 mins (you cook in batches)** MAKES **about 18–20 puffs**

INGREDIENTS

125ml (4½fl oz) water

125ml (4½fl oz) milk

75g (3oz) butter, cubed

½ tsp salt, plus extra for sprinkling

½ tsp white pepper

110g (4oz) plain flour

3 eggs, beaten

75g (3oz) Emmental cheese, grated

Vegetable oil, for frying

METHOD

§   Add the water, milk, butter, salt and white pepper to a saucepan and place over a medium heat. Bring the liquid to the boil then reduce the heat and add the flour.

§   Beat the mixture with a wooden spoon until a dough is formed that leaves the sides of the pan and forms a ball. Slowly start to beat in the beaten egg a little at a time. You may not need it all; you want a thick, silky dough that will drop from the spoon on the count of five.

§   Then beat in the grated cheese. Keep the mix to one side.

§   Heat the oil to 180°C (350°F) in a deep frying pan – use a cook's thermometer to be precise. When the oil is ready, take two dessertspoons and use them to shape balls of dough. Carefully lower the balls into the fat and cook for 5–6 minutes until a beautiful golden brown. You will need to fry them in batches, so as to maintain the temperature of the oil. Use a metal slotted spoon to help them turn in the oil so they cook evenly.

§   Scoop out the cooked puffs using the slotted spoon and drain on kitchen paper, then sprinkle over a little salt. Serve them immediately.

PARTY DRINKS

HIGHCLERE CHRISTMAS COCKTAIL

This pretty, light drink is enervating and full of Christmas colour. It is a great favourite whenever we entertain during festivities at the Castle.

INGREDIENTS

FOR THE SPICED SYRUP
250ml (9fl oz) cold water
120g (4¼oz) caster sugar
3 cinnamon sticks
4 whole cloves
Peel of ¼ orange

FOR THE COCKTAIL
35ml (1¼fl oz) cranberry
   juice
Red sugar (see tip)
50ml (2fl oz) spiced syrup
Highclere Champagne
   (or any good champagne)

METHOD

§   First make the syrup. Put the cold water, sugar, cinnamon sticks, cloves and orange peel into a saucepan, then bring to a boil over a low heat, stirring gently.

§   Let the mixture reduce until you achieve a syrupy texture (about 5 minutes once boiled).

§   Remove the cinnamon, cloves and orange peel and leave to cool.

§   To make the cocktail, dip the rim of a Champagne flute into cranberry juice and then into the red sugar.

§   Put the syrup and the rest of the cranberry juice into the glass and top up with Champagne.

[CHEF'S TIP: Coloured sugar is readily available to buy, or you can make it yourself by simply mixing food colouring and sugar.]

CHRISTMAS CHAMPAGNE COCKTAIL

A simple, but utterly reliable crowd-pleaser.

INGREDIENTS
25ml (1fl oz) Cointreau
50ml (2fl oz)
   cranberry juice
Highclere Champagne
   (or any good champagne)
Twist of orange peel,
   to garnish

METHOD

§   Pour the Cointreau and the cranberry juice into a flute glass and top up with Champagne.

§   Garnish with a twist of orange peel.

DRESSED CRAB

Family Christmases in Cornwall involved regular visits to Port Isaac to watch the fishing boats come in from the rolling seas to safety within the harbour walls. Crabs are at their best in the winter months and caught in traditional ink-well-shaped crab pots, which used to be constructed from willow withies, although I suspect that has changed now. My father would navigate his car down and park on the beach before strolling in to inspect what might be delicious for supper.

PREPARATION TIME 60 mins   COOKING TIME 15 mins   SERVES 4

INGREDIENTS

4 whole crabs

Lemon juice, to taste, plus wedges to serve

Salt and pepper

Chopped parsley/chervil, to serve

METHOD

§   Place each crab into a large pan of boiling water. While the crabs are cooking, prepare an ice bath by filling a large bowl with cold water and ice. Allow each crab to cook for about 15 minutes, then place in the iced water.

§   Pull off the claws and legs and then, with the crab's body on its back and facing away from you, bring your thumbs up under the rear edge and push firmly to lift out the core. Remove the dead man's fingers from around the core. Crack the claws with the heel of your knife to obtain as much of the white meat as possible. Dig your thumb in behind the eyes and mouthparts and lift out the bony and gooey bits – these are the inedible parts of the digestive tract. Scoop everything else out of the shell into a bowl.

§   Add salt and black pepper, lemon juice to taste, and combine it to a paste, then spoon the mixture back into the washed shell.

§   Spoon the white meat into the shell, either side of the brown meat.

§   Serve scattered with chopped parsley/chervil and with a lemon wedge and a dressed green salad.

SALMON EN CROÛTE

Undoubtedly an impressive dish, it is a good marriage of a poached salmon steaming inside the pastry and thus it should not dry out. It is a nice change from meat dishes and reassuringly comforting.

PREPARATION TIME 20 mins   COOKING TIME 45 mins, plus cooling   SERVES 6–8

INGREDIENTS

20g (¾oz) unsalted butter

3 banana shallots, finely chopped

400g (14oz) spinach, washed

Zest of 2 lemons

1kg (2¼lb) salmon fillet, skinned, pinned and trimmed

500g (1lb 2oz) block of puff pastry

Flour, for dusting

1 egg, beaten

Salt and pepper

200g (7oz) watercress, to serve

METHOD

§   Preheat the oven to 210°C/410°F/Gas mark 6.

§   Place the butter in a large saucepan over a medium heat and sauté the shallots for 5 minutes until softened. Add the spinach to the pan and cook until it is wilted. This will probably take 5–7 minutes. Remove from the heat and transfer to a sieve. Press the spinach with a wooden spoon to squeeze out any excess water, then transfer to a mixing bowl. Add the lemon zest and some seasoning.

§   Place the salmon on a chopping board and cut it in half. Rub the cut side of a lemon over the top side. Cover the one piece of salmon with the cooked spinach and put the other piece of salmon on top to make an oversized salmon sandwich.

§   Roll out the puff pastry on a lightly floured worktop to approximately the thickness of a pound coin and to a size that will encase the salmon pieces. Then place the pastry on a lined baking sheet ready for the oven (this is so you don't have to move the salmon again). Place the salmon on one half of the puff pastry, leaving a good 2·5cm (1 inch) border on three sides. Brush this border with a little of the beaten egg.

§   Fold the pastry over the salmon, gently shaping it around the fish and squeezing out the air, then press down on all the edges to seal and trim off any excess pastry.

§   Use the rest of the beaten egg to glaze the pastry and decorate by scoring with a knife.

§   Place in the oven and bake for 20–25 minutes, 30 if you like your fish fully cooked through. Allow to rest for 10 minutes before carving and serving with fresh watercress.

STRAWBERRY AND SHERRY TRIFLE

My husband asks for trifle from time to time as it reminds him of eating in the Castle as a child. He thought it was a great excitement to have a pudding with a strong taste of alcohol. It is a very English pudding with layers of fruit, jelly, custard and tipsy sponge. Do not trifle with the trifle – it is a great traditional pudding.

PREPARATION TIME 30 mins   COOKING TIME 1 hour, plus setting and chilling   SERVES 8–10

INGREDIENTS

FOR THE SPONGE
250g (9oz) softened butter
250g (9oz) caster sugar
250g (9oz) self-raising flour
4 eggs
Pinch of salt
Splash of milk

FOR THE CUSTARD
350ml (12fl oz) full-fat milk
Seeds from 1 vanilla pod or
   dash of vanilla extract
4 egg yolks
60g (2½oz) caster sugar
20g (¾oz) cornflour

FOR THE TRIFLE
Sherry, to taste
600g (1lb 5oz) strawberries,
   hulled and sliced
400ml (14fl oz)
   strawberry jelly
   (made up from a packet)
400ml (14fl oz)
   double cream

METHOD

§   Preheat the oven to 180°C/350°F/Gas mark 4 and grease and line a 20cm (8 inch) cake tin.

§   First make the sponge. Cream together the butter and sugar in a food processor.

§   Add the flour and eggs in alternate batches until all incorporated. Add the salt and enough milk to achieve a 'dropping' consistency (where the batter will slowly drop from a spoon under its own gravity).

§   Transfer the sponge batter to the cake tin and bake for about 22 minutes, until golden and pulling away from the sides of the cake tin.

§   Remove from the oven and allow to cool before removing from the tin, then leave to cool completely on a wire rack. Once cool, roughly cut the cake into chunks.

§   Meanwhile, prepare the custard. Place the milk and vanilla in a pan over a moderate heat; do not boil.

§   Beat the egg yolks, sugar and cornflour together until quite pale and thick in a mixing bowl. Pour in half the warm milk and combine. Then add the rest.

§   Return the egg mix to the pan and continue to heat until it thickens. Stir continuously to avoid sticking or burning. Transfer to a clean dish and allow to cool thoroughly.

§   Line the base of your chosen serving dish (or individual dishes) with rough chunks of sponge. Pour over the sherry to soften the sponge, being careful not to drown it (unless you like a very wet trifle!).

§   Cover the sponge with half of the strawberries, then pour over the jelly and transfer to the fridge to set.

§   While the jelly sets, whip the cream to very soft peaks. When the jelly is firm enough, pour over the custard, then spoon over the whipped cream (if you have time, use a piping bag fitted with a star nozzle) and finish with the remaining strawberries.

CHAPTER NINE

F E A S T S

❧ JUST ONE LETTER MAKES ❧ ALL THE DIFFERENCE AND TRANSFORMS

A *FAST* INTO A *FEAST*. TRADITIONALLY THE PERIOD before Christmas, Advent, was a time of fasting, perhaps a practical idea given that food and resources would have been in short supply. In fact, the word 'fast' is rooted in the Anglo-Saxon language and means to hold fast or to stand firm. However, when Christmas arrives and we are confronted with the most delicious dishes, as well as the extra letter, it is time for feasting, goodwill and joy as we make merry with an abundance of food.

23 DECEMBER

BY THIS TIME, THERE IS A SENSE OF QUIET EXCITEMENT as preparations for Christmas in the Castle are largely complete. Housekeeper Diana and her team will have made up beds, aired rooms and stocked bathrooms with towels, bathrobes, soaps and everything else one might need for a luxuriant soak in the deep, old-fashioned baths we have in the Castle.

The Castle bedrooms do not have any modern heating but the bedroom doors are left open to the gallery, which does have a few night storage heaters, and the warm air circulates, we like to imagine, into the bedrooms. As a practical concession to warmth, where once fires would have been laid by housemaids, a panel radiator stands in each bedroom fireplace ready to be plugged in, if needed.

Diana keeps the shutters and curtains closed to insulate the rooms as much as possible before guests arrive laden with suitcases and parcels to add to the already large piles of presents under the tree.

All incidental checks to lights, radios, dressing tables and cupboards made and completed, the house stands quiet with only the fire crackling in the Saloon and the sounds of distant footsteps, or doors opening and closing, indicating behind-the-scenes 'busyness'.

It was ever thus – family and friends travelling from near and far, to join and enjoy the festive season. Howard Carter wrote in *The Tomb of Tutankhamun: Volume 1*, of Lord Carnarvon's return to Highclere at Christmas:

Those who travelled with him [the 5th Earl] on his annual journey — or progress rather — from Paddington to Highclere at Christmas

RIGHT
Muffet the miniature Shetland waits patiently by the picnic at the Etruscan Temple

*can never forget the warmth his presence called forth in the railway
employees of all grades, from inspectors to engine drivers. The festival
gave them and him an opportunity of expressing their feeling, their
genuine feeling for one another. It is no exaggeration to say that it was
a moving scene, singularly appropriate to the celebration of the great
family feast of the year.*

To help keep the house tidy before the bulk of the guests arrive that
evening, and just for fun, lunch today is a picnic by the Etruscan Temple.

Luis and Jorge, our Portuguese banqueting team, thoroughly approve
of the British love of port but fail entirely to understand our preoccupation
with picnics, given our climate. I remain eternally optimistic, so the trestle
table is set and Muffet the Shetland pony will join us as an amusement
for my nieces, being a much better option than the Labradors, who might
mistake our picnic for theirs.

RIGHT
Muffet in festive finery

This particular temple was a folly originally built in the mid-eighteenth century in a natural amphitheatre in the woods. Neglected, I suspect it was the 4th Earl who decided to reposition it a mile away in its new high vantage point. By our turn, it had again become somewhat 'lost', so Geordie and I have cleared the grassy terraces below it to highlight a more formal setting for a folly which invokes a classical style.

It can easily be overlooked, yet this little temple reflects Etruscan architecture, with columns made from wood, the low-pitched roof with terracotta tiles protecting three sides of the little building and a strong frontal design. Given our climate, there is little decoration on its exterior but there are plaster friezes inside which really allude to the Greeks, with figures and riders. Given the Etruscan temples were often used as tombs, it is entirely appropriate that there are some stones propped outside with names of beloved dogs engraved on them.

The temple overlooks one of the most beautiful views across the park to the south. Inspiring a tranquillity of mind, the eye follows the broad sweeps of parkland punctuated by Cedars of Lebanon to one side which catch the rays and cast their shadows from the setting sun. To the other side, the park is flanked by the tall silhouettes of the bare lime trees with mistletoe clustered in globes amongst the branches, whilst glancing up, the outline of Heaven's Gate is clearly silhouetted on the summit of Siddown Hill.

The stone seats inside the little temple need a few cushions, and if there were a dress code for this picnic, it would be warm coats, sensible shoes, scarves and hats. Forgiving of English eccentricity, Luis and team load the red truck with trestle tables, chairs and cushions, which they drive along to the temple to set up ready for the food. Muffet the Shetland pony and friends and family wander along, delighted by the novelty.

LADY
CARNARVON'S
CHRISTMAS
QUICHE
is a perfect picnic dish
PAGE 178

AS A GREAT ADMIRER OF JANE AUSTEN, I KNOW THAT 23 December was the day her novel *Emma* was published, in 1815, which takes place around the fictional village of Highbury, rather than Highclere, although a few years after her death, her nephew the Revd J. Edward Austen (later Austen Leigh) became Curate of nearby Newtown, appointed by the Rector of Burghclere, the 2nd Earl's brother George Herbert.

The protagonists set off for a supper party on a wintry evening just before Christmas, despite their qualms because, as one character, Mr Elton says,

> *this is quite the season indeed for friendly meetings. At Christmas everybody invites their friends about them, and people think little of even the worst weather.*

Emma's father, Mr Woodhouse, took all precautions against chills, wrapping up well and they all enjoyed an amusing evening. I hope my guests feel the same.

As the afternoon light falls, all at Highclere settle in to a peaceful evening sitting round the fire. It is a good time to begin a jigsaw puzzle, or unearth the old games and boards. Gathering by the fire in the Saloon, family and friends nestle into cosy corners of rooms, looking forward to supper. Thus Highclere's Christmas begins. We raise a toast – a glass of champagne – to celebrate everyone's safe arrival.

LADY CARNARVON'S FENNEL, BLOOD ORANGE AND WALNUT SALAD

I am always looking for colourful salads to offer in winter, and equally I often use nuts to give a little energy boost at this time of year, when it is most needed.

I was lucky enough to be asked to explore an orange grove in Sicily and I have never forgotten the experience of just picking an orange and standing eating the extraordinary luscious fruit straight from the tree – nothing has ever tasted quite so good. Sicilian oranges are, of course, exported over here, and are delicious, but given the time spent in transport and storage, they cannot have the same overflowing taste.

Blood oranges need the cool fall in night temperatures to create their vivid colour, which looks sensational in Christmas salads or puddings.

Another key ingredient here is fennel – not everyone likes fennel, but I do. It was thought to help with eyesight, and Henry Longfellow wrote about it thus:

Above the lower plants it towers, / The Fennel with its yellow flowers;
And in an earlier age than ours / Was gifted with the wondrous powers / Lost vision to restore.

PREPARATION TIME **20 mins**   COOKING TIME **5 mins**   SERVES **4**

INGREDIENTS

2 fennel bulbs
2 large blood oranges
20ml (¾fl oz) walnut oil
60g (2½oz) walnuts
120g (4¼oz) rocket, washed
Sea salt and cracked black pepper

METHOD

§ Peel and wash the whole fennel bulbs. Cut straight down the middle of each and remove the hearts – the hard centre near the root. Slice the bulbs as thinly as you can (we use a mandoline for this).

§ Peel the blood oranges and divide into segments, saving any juice for use in the dressing. Squeeze the pulp left from the segments to extract a little more.

§ Place a frying pan over a high heat and add half the walnut oil. When hot, carefully add the walnuts and fry until nicely toasted on both sides. Remove the nuts from the pan and allow to cool.

§ Combine the rocket, walnuts and fennel in a big serving bowl. Dress with the remaining walnut oil and the juice from the oranges and gently toss everything together – try not to handle the salad too much. Season with cracked black pepper and sea salt, then divide among individual serving bowls and distribute the blood orange segments between them.

AUBERGINE AND POMEGRANATE SALAD

This colourful salad is a light, fresh dish – perfect after a lot of rich food over Christmas.

PREPARATION TIME 10 mins   COOKING TIME 40 mins   SERVES 4

INGREDIENTS

2 aubergines

4 good Italian tomatoes
 (San Marzano), quartered

2 red peppers,
 de-seeded and diced

2–3 spring onions,
 thinly sliced

Seeds from 1 pomegranate

A handful of mint, chopped

FOR THE DRESSING

4 tbsp extra virgin olive oil

2 tbsp pomegranate
 molasses

Juice of 1 lemon
 (as much as you like)

Salt and pepper

METHOD

§   Preheat the oven to 200°C/400°F/Gas mark 6.

§   Line a roasting tin with tin foil. Pierce the aubergines with a knife in a few places, then roast for 50 minutes until wrinkled and soft. Set to one side until cool enough to handle.

§   When the aubergine is cool, carefully peel off the skin and leave to rest on kitchen paper to absorb any juices. Cut the flesh into large pieces and place on your serving plate. Add the tomatoes, peppers, spring onions, pomegranate seeds and the chopped mint.

§   Make the dressing by whisking together the extra virgin olive oil, pomegranate molasses and as much lemon juice as suits your taste. Season with some salt and pepper before pouring over the salad and serving immediately.

LADY CARNARVON'S CHRISTMAS QUICHE

This is delicious hot or cold and whilst here it is served as part of lunch, it is also a good supper dish with a green salad.

PREPARATION TIME 25 mins, plus chilling and cooling   COOKING TIME 25 mins   SERVES 6–8

INGREDIENTS

FOR THE PASTRY

250g (9oz) plain flour,
  plus extra for dusting
125g (4½oz) cold butter,
  diced
Pinch of salt
1 egg yolk
2 tbsp cold water

FOR THE FILLING

5 eggs
150ml (5fl oz) double cream
1 tsp English mustard
175g (6oz) brie,
  cut into pieces
125g (4½oz) fresh
  cranberries (or you
  can use dried, soaked for
  15 minutes in cold water)
Salt and pepper

METHOD

§   Start by making the pastry. Blitz the flour, butter and salt in a food processor until it resembles breadcrumbs, then decant into a mixing bowl. Mix the egg yolk with the cold water and add just enough of it to the flour mix to make a pastry dough – it should hold together but not be sticky. Use your hands to shape it into a flat round, then wrap the pastry in cling film and chill for 30 minutes in the fridge.

§   When chilled, roll out the pastry on a lightly floured worktop to the thickness of a pound coin, then carefully lift it into a 25cm (10 inch) loose-bottomed, fluted tart tin.

§   Use a little piece of the pastry to press the pastry into all the corners and up the sides of the tin.

§   Put the tin in the fridge for 15 minutes.

§   Preheat the oven to 190°C/375°F/Gas mark 5.

§   Cover the pastry with baking paper and fill with baking beans (or dry rice), then blind bake for 12 minutes. Remove the paper and return the pastry case to the oven for a further 8 minutes.

§   Meanwhile, use a hand whisk to blend the eggs, cream, mustard and some seasoning. Pour this into the pastry case. Scatter the brie and cranberries evenly over the egg mix.

§   Place the tart in the oven and bake for 20–25 minutes or until the quiche is firm but has a very slight wobble in the centre.

§   Allow to cool for 10 minutes before removing from the tin, then enjoy immediately, or chill and consume within 3 days.

[CHEF'S TIP: You might like to add cold diced meats to this dish (turkey, ham, etc.) but it remains very tasty without.]

WINTER FRUIT SALAD

This is a marvellous store-cupboard pudding that can be made ahead of time.

PREPARATION TIME **15 mins**   COOKING TIME **10 mins, plus resting**   SERVES 6–8

INGREDIENTS

150ml (5fl oz) maple syrup

100ml (3½fl oz) apple juice (or cider)

200g (7oz) dried red plums or 100g (3½oz) dried cranberries

100g (3½oz) dried apricots

100g (3½oz) Agen prunes, pitted

200g (7oz) dried figs

100g (3½oz) Medjool dates, pitted

Zest and juice of 1 lemon

Zest and juice of 1 orange

1 tsp ground cinnamon

½ tsp ground allspice

2 tbsp cider brandy or Calvados (optional)

Greek yoghurt, to serve

METHOD

§   Place all the ingredients, with the alcohol if using, in a large saucepan. Bring to a gentle simmer then turn off the heat.

§   Leave overnight for the fruit to swell.

§   Serve with a spoonful of Greek yoghurt.

§   This pudding keeps for several days in the fridge.

CHRISTMAS EVE

IF CHRISTMAS DAY, ABOVE ALL, IS A TIME TO GATHER together and enjoy a 'feast', Christmas Eve is without doubt all about children and Santa Claus in all his guises. This is when all the carefully thought-out planning and distribution of gifts reaches its apogee.

By 4pm in the afternoon there is really not much more that any grown-up can achieve, and thus it is time for tea. Noël Coward commented, 'Wouldn't it be dreadful to live in a country where they didn't have tea?' In general, outside Britain as well as within the grand hotels, the tradition of afternoon tea has undoubtedly enjoyed a renaissance recently, although I am not sure it ever was not part of Highclere's day.

The tea is set up between the Christmas tree and the fire in the Saloon, and as friends and family materialise, more plates are brought out, laden with choice. Geordie cuts into the Christmas cake, picking off the hardened white icing to taste it and slicing out the cake whilst trying to avoid the marzipan. Nanny ticks him off and eats the marzipan. Others find the sandwiches enticing, whilst I find the banana bread hard to resist, although it is the actual cup of tea which I enjoy and savour most.

After tea comes Geordie's most important task of the day. Sitting in a comfy, deep, red armchair in the Library, with the little ones listening, he prepares to read the classic Christmas poem that his father used to read to him. As the fire blazes, inevitably much of the rest of the house party settles in as well in the various sofas and chairs, with the occasional dog squeezing between children sitting on the floor, nuzzling for attention and tickles.

Geordie begins his narration with much dramatic enthusiasm, although it is not long before his delivery is either interrupted by heckles, or dogs to tell off, or over-eager audience participation.

'Twas the Night before Christmas was written by an American scholar, Clement Clarke Moore. Geordie's grandmother was from the Moore family of New York, and I wonder if he might be related to the man who helped create such a jolly figure and myth. This particular image also borrows much from an illustration, 'A visit from St Nicholas' by Thomas Nast for *Harper's Weekly*, in 1863, which mirrors this poem.

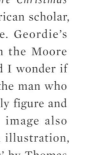

Recipes for everything that goes to make a delicious
CHRISTMAS EVE TEA
begin on PAGE 186

A VISIT FROM ST NICHOLAS

'Twas the night before Christmas, when all through the house
Not a creature was stirring, not even a mouse;
The stockings were hung by the chimney with care,
In hopes that St Nicholas soon would be there;
The children were nestled all snug in their beds,
While visions of sugar-plums danced in their heads;
And mamma in her 'kerchief, and I in my cap,
Had just settled down for a long winter's nap,
When out on the lawn there arose such a clatter,
I sprang from the bed to see what was the matter.
Away to the window I flew like a flash,
Tore open the shutters and threw up the sash.
The moon on the breast of the new-fallen snow
Gave the lustre of mid-day to objects below,
When, what to my wondering eyes should appear,
But a miniature sleigh, and eight tiny reindeer,
With a little old driver, so lively and quick,
I knew in a moment it must be St Nick.
More rapid than eagles his coursers they came,
And he whistled, and shouted, and called them by name;
'Now, DASHER! now, DANCER! now, PRANCER and VIXEN!
On, COMET! on CUPID! on, DONNER and BLITZEN!
To the top of the porch! to the top of the wall!
Now dash away! dash away! dash away all!'
As dry leaves that before the wild hurricane fly,
When they meet with an obstacle, mount to the sky,
So up to the house-top the coursers they flew,
With the sleigh full of toys, and St Nicholas too.

And then, in a twinkling, I heard on the roof
The prancing and pawing of each little hoof.
As I drew in my hand, and was turning around,
Down the chimney St Nicholas came with a bound.
He was dressed all in fur, from his head to his foot,
And his clothes were all tarnished with ashes and soot;
A bundle of toys he had flung on his back,
And he looked like a pedlar just opening his pack.
His eyes -- how they twinkled! his dimples how merry!
His cheeks were like roses, his nose like a cherry!
His droll little mouth was drawn up like a bow,
And the beard of his chin was as white as the snow;
The stump of a pipe he held tight in his teeth,
And the smoke it encircled his head like a wreath;
He had a broad face and a little round belly,
That shook, when he laughed like a bowlful of jelly.
He was chubby and plump, a right jolly old elf,
And I laughed when I saw him, in spite of myself;
A wink of his eye and a twist of his head,
Soon gave me to know I had nothing to dread;
He spoke not a word, but went straight to his work,
And filled all the stockings; then turned with a jerk,
And laying his finger aside of his nose,
And giving a nod, up the chimney he rose;
He sprang to his sleigh, to his team gave a whistle,
And away they all flew like the down of a thistle.
But I heard him exclaim, ere he drove out of sight,
HAPPY CHRISTMAS TO ALL, AND TO ALL A GOOD-NIGHT!

CLEMENT CLARKE MOORE

FATHER CHRISTMAS

CHRISTMAS EVE NIGHT IS NEARLY UPON US, AND WHO is not excited at the thought that Father Christmas will fly across the sky on a sleigh pulled by reindeer, hardly able to steer because the sleigh is piled so high with gifts.

The origins of Santa Claus, or Father Christmas, can be traced back through the centuries from Odin in Norse mythology, to Saint Nicholas in the fourth century, through to the Dutch Sinterklaas. St Nicholas became the patron saint of Russia and Greece and variously of children, sailors and other charitable guilds, but his association with gift-giving to children – whether naughty or nice – developed primarily in the nineteenth and twentieth centuries.

Highclere has rather a lot of chimneys, but hopefully Father Christmas will choose the right one. The chimney in the Saloon is best as it is regularly swept and we let the fire go out early on this night so that it is also cool. As the more junior members of the house party depart for bed, they help arrange glasses of brandy or whisky and plenty of mince pies for Father Christmas, not forgetting, of course, the carrots (with tops) for the reindeer, who will have to wait on the roof. Luis will consult Nanny as to what particular tipple she thinks Father Christmas might enjoy – who knew he had a penchant for Baileys Irish Cream?

Much later, as most retire to bed, Nanny can be found happily ensconced in one of the Saloon armchairs, waiting up to greet Father Christmas. The house falls silent, apart from the regular ticking and occasional chimes of the Saloon longcase clock.

Tucked up in bed, the imagination can roam because tonight, 24 December, is when the spirits rove. The Scandinavians, with their Viking heritage and dark winters, do not go out at all on this night for fear they may bump into trolls, witches or even hobgoblins. At Highclere, as the lights go out, it is easy to imagine spirits and ghosts hovering outside around the yew trees, so it is better not to talk, instead to fall asleep and know that Father Christmas, with his bells, sleigh and bonhomie, will disperse the ghosts as he travels through the night.

LEFT
Nanny awaits Father
Christmas's arrival with
a glass of Baileys and a
mince pie

CHRISTMAS EVE TEA

For tea on Christmas Eve we have a selection of cakes and delicate finger sandwiches. The fillings included here work well and tend to please most palates.

For all the sandwiches, cut off the crusts from the bread with a very sharp knife, and slice into three fingers. Display the sandwiches on their side as they are so colourful – and it also makes it easier for people to choose which ones they prefer! Each recipe serves 4–6.

MOZZARELLA AND ROASTED PEPPER

A very colourful and flavourful (vegetarian) combination.

INGREDIENTS

A handful of rocket,
  rinsed and dried
250g (9oz) mozzarella,
  thinly sliced
250g (9oz) roasted red peppers
  (roast and skin these yourself
  or take advantage of the very
  good ones you can get in
  jars), sliced
8 slices good Italian bread
  (such as Focaccia, page 108)
Salt and pepper

METHOD

§   Layer the rocket, mozzarella slices and roasted red peppers on four of the bread slices.

§   Season with salt and pepper, to taste, and top with the remaining bread slices.

TURKEY AND CRANBERRY SAUCE

The classic Christmas leftover combination.

INGREDIENTS

8 slices multigrain bread
(or do half wholemeal,
half white)

40g (1½oz) butter, softened

30g (1¼oz) baby spinach

200g (7oz) leftover turkey
breast, thinly sliced

30g (1¼oz) cranberry sauce

Salt and pepper

METHOD

§ Spread each bread slice with butter. Divide the spinach between the slices and top with the turkey. Season to taste, then spread the remaining bread slices with cranberry sauce and place on top of the turkey, sauce-side down. You can add a little leftover turkey stuffing to the sandwiches, too, if you like.

POACHED SALMON AND WATERCRESS

The cool, soft salmon contrasts so well with the crisp, peppery watercress.

INGREDIENTS

FOR THE SALMON
1 tsp salt
3 tbsp white wine vinegar
500g (1lb 2oz) salmon fillet

FOR THE SANDWICHES
8 slices wholemeal bread
40g (1½oz) butter, softened
Mayonnaise (optional)
Handful of watercress,
   rinsed and dried
Black pepper

METHOD

§   Measure 7·5cm (3 inches) of water into a wide-rimmed saucepan. Add the salt and white wine vinegar and bring to a boil. Once boiling, add the salmon, turn the heat to a low simmer and cook gently for 6–7 minutes. The fish should feel slightly springy and the flesh will be translucent. It's important not to overcook salmon, but even if you do it still makes wonderful sandwiches.

§   Remove the salmon from the pan with a slotted spatula. Cool it on a plate lined with kitchen paper to absorb the liquid.

§   Lay out the slices of bread and butter each slice. Spread mayonnaise (if using) on half the slices.

§   Place some salmon on four of the slices of bread, lay the watercress on top of the salmon and grind a little black pepper over.

§   Lay the other slices of bread over the top and press down lightly.

MINI VICTORIA SPONGES

You could use this recipe to make one big cake, but mini Victoria sponges look very sweet and do not take long to cook. If you are serving them on a plate you can decorate them with a few raspberries or redcurrants scattered around them and dust them with icing sugar.

PREPARATION TIME **15 mins**   COOKING TIME **20–22 mins**   MAKES **12**

INGREDIENTS

100g (3½oz) butter,
  plus extra for greasing
110g (4oz) caster sugar
2 eggs, beaten
125g (4½oz)
  self-raising flour
Pinch of salt
½ tsp vanilla extract
Splash of milk

FOR THE FILLING
50g (2oz) softened butter
120g (4¼oz) icing sugar,
  plus extra for dusting
Vanilla extract, to taste
Strawberry jam
  (or whatever is your
  favourite jam)

METHOD

§   Preheat the oven to 180°C/350°F/Gas mark 4.

§   Grease a 12-hole baking tin and line each cup with a collar made from a 20 × 6cm (8 × 2½ inch) strip of baking paper. Place to one side.

§   Blend the butter and sugar with an electric whisk until light in colour and fluffy in texture.

§   Add the beaten eggs slowly to the butter and sugar.

§   Sift the flour and salt together and incorporate into the mixture.

§   Add the vanilla and milk to achieve 'dropping' consistency (see page 167). Transfer the mix to a piping bag and pipe 60g (2½oz) of cake batter into each mould.

§   Place the baking tray in the centre of the oven for 20–22 minutes, until golden and well risen.

§   Remove from the oven and allow to cool for 10 minutes in the tin. Then carefully remove the cakes and transfer to a wire rack to cool fully.

§   Meanwhile, make a buttercream by beating the butter, icing sugar and vanilla extract together.

§   When the cakes are cool, remove them carefully from their collars and cut each in half horizontally.

§   Spread jam on each bottom half, buttercream on the top half, reassemble and dust with icing sugar.

YULE LOG

This is fun to make and if you do so with children it will create rather a mess! The sponge should be light and whichever bits are not perfectly rolled can be accounted for as bark and twigs with redcurrants, blueberries and sprigs of holly, but please make sure the holly or any other garden plant you use for decoration has absolutely no berries on it.

PREPARATION TIME 40 mins   COOKING TIME 20 mins, plus cooling and decorating   SERVES 10–12

INGREDIENTS

FOR THE CAKE

6 large eggs, separated
150g (5oz) caster sugar
1 tsp ground cinnamon
120g (4¼oz) plain flour
50g (2oz) good-quality
    cocoa powder, sifted

FOR THE FILLING AND ICING

1 tbsp vanilla extract
150ml (5fl oz) double cream,
    whipped
75g (3oz) dark chocolate
    (70%), broken into
    chunks
225g (8oz) soft butter
250g (9oz) icing sugar,
    sifted, plus extra for
    dusting

METHOD

§   Preheat the oven to 180°C/350°F/Gas mark 4.

§   Use an electric whisk to beat the egg whites in a large glass bowl until they are thick and standing up. Sprinkle in 50g (2oz) of the caster sugar and whisk again.

§   In another bowl, whisk the egg yolks and the remaining caster sugar until creamy and thick. Add the cinnamon and fold in the flour and cocoa powder.

§   Use a large metal spoon and fold the egg whites into the egg yolks in stages.

§   Line a Swiss roll tin with baking paper, but do not trim it too tightly. Pour in the cake mixture and bake in the oven for 20–22 minutes or until just cooked through and springy to the touch.

§   Let the cake cool a little before turning it out onto another piece of baking paper. Cover with a clean tea towel to keep it soft.

§   Stir the vanilla into the whipped cream. Melt the chocolate slowly in a bain-marie, then take off the heat. In another bowl, beat the butter with a mixer until pale, then gradually add the icing sugar and cool melted chocolate. Carefully spoon a thin covering of the chocolate icing over the cake, then spoon the whipped cream across. Roll up the cake carefully and leave the paper wrapped around it as it settles.

§   Sprinkle a wooden board with icing sugar, unwrap the cake and place it on the board, then cut off a small diagonal at one end. Cover the whole thing with the remaining chocolate icing and score it carefully with a fork so it resembles tree bark. Arrange the cut-off 'twig' at an angle to the main log and cover with icing.

§   Place some green holly around the board and cake and use a few redcurrants or blueberries to look like berries.

BANANA LOAF

In *Proverbs in the English Tongue* (1546), John Heywood notes that 'wolde you bothe eate your cake, and have your cake?' – i.e. once you have eaten it, it is no longer there, thus it is not possible to have two good things at the same time. However, a banana loaf is both to have and to eat.

This recipe is a good way of using over-ripe bananas and the loaf (or bread, given it is made in a bread-shaped tin) remains deliciously moist.

PREPARATION TIME **20 mins**   COOKING TIME **about 1 hr**   SERVES **8–10**

INGREDIENTS

280g (10oz) plain flour
1 tsp bicarbonate of soda
½ tsp mixed spice
½ tsp ground cinnamon
½ tsp salt
110g (4oz) butter, plus extra
  for greasing
225g (8oz) caster sugar
2 eggs
4 ripe bananas, mashed
85ml (3¼fl oz) buttermilk
1 tsp vanilla extract

FOR THE GARNISH

25g (1oz) caster sugar
½ tsp vanilla essence
1–2 tbsp hot water
1 banana, peeled and halved
a few walnut halves
knob of butter
Whipped cream

METHOD

§   Preheat the oven to 180°C/350°F/Gas mark 4 and grease and line a 450g (1lb) loaf tin.

§   Sift the flour, bicarbonate of soda, spices and salt into a large mixing bowl.

§   In a separate bowl, cream the butter and sugar together until light and fluffy.

§   Add the eggs, mashed bananas, buttermilk and vanilla extract to the butter and sugar mixture and mix well. Fold in the flour mixture.

§   Pour the cake mixture into the loaf tin. Transfer to the oven and bake for about an hour, or until well-risen, golden brown and a skewer inserted into the cake comes out clean.

§   Remove from the oven and cool in the tin for a few minutes, then turn out onto a wire rack to cool completely.

§   The cake is delicious on its own, but if you would like to add a spectacular garnish heat the sugar, vanilla essence and water in a pan, until it forms a caramel.

§   Add the banana halves and walnuts to the pan, shaking to coat. Add the butter to the pan and heat for another 1–2 minutes. Remove from the pan and allow to cool completely.

§   Just before serving, decorate the cake with as much whipped cream as you like, topped with the caramelised banana and nuts.

SEVILLE ORANGE POLENTA CAKE

A polenta cake adds an Italian twist to afternoon tea. Polenta is a type of corn from northern Italy that can be used in many dishes – it is a real comfort food. It also makes anyone who prefers to avoid wheat flour very happy. This version is married to the Christmas-time pleasure of Seville oranges; I enjoy the texture of the polenta, and the cake stays lovely and syrupy. I find I have to taste half a slice and then the other half, which means, of course, eating far less than a whole slice.

PREPARATION TIME 10 mins   COOKING TIME 1 hr 25 mins, plus cooling   SERVES 8–10

INGREDIENTS

2 Seville oranges

2 lemons

4 eggs

Pinch of salt

175g (6oz) caster sugar

180g (6¼oz) ground almonds

80ml (3¼oz) olive oil, plus extra for greasing

150g (5oz) polenta

10g (¼oz) baking powder (use gluten-free variety if needed)

FOR THE SYRUP

150ml (5fl oz) fresh orange juice

75g (3oz) caster sugar

METHOD

§   Preheat the oven to 180°C/350°F/Gas mark 4 and grease and line a 22cm (9 inch) springform cake tin.

§   Put 1 orange and 1 lemon into a pan and cover with cold water. Place a circle of baking paper (cartouche) on top to keep the fruit submerged. Bring to the boil, then reduce the heat and simmer for 30 minutes. Remove the cooked fruit from the pan, cut in half and remove the pips.

§   Juice the remaining orange and lemon, and add to a food processor with the cooked fruit (skin and all) and blitz to form a paste.

§   In a large bowl, beat the eggs with the salt until foaming. Add the sugar and beat again. Then add the orange/lemon paste, almonds and olive oil. Beat again.

§   In a separate bowl, mix the polenta and baking powder, then gently fold into the mixture.

§   Pour the mixture into the tin and bake for 40–45 minutes or until a skewer inserted into the middle comes out clean.

§   While the cake is cooking, make the syrup. Put the orange juice and sugar into a pan and simmer over a low heat until you have a glossy syrup. When the cake is still warm, pour the syrup over it so that it is all absorbed.

§   Garnish as you like. Some fine slices of orange, shreds of candied orange zest (see page 139 for how to make these), and attractive dry spices such as cinnamon sticks or star anise are all good. And if you are feeling very indulgent, clotted cream will do no harm.

CHRISTMAS DAY

AS CHRISTMAS DAY DAWNS, I DRAW THE CURTAINS AND fold back the shutters to see if by any chance there might be a dusting of snow or, the more likely, a pristine sprinkling of frost across the lawns.

I can hear nephews and nieces excitedly running barefoot along corridors between bedrooms to compare the overnight haul that's been left at the end of each bed. I remember that same childish excitement so well. As children, my sisters and I used to put out pillowcases – I suspect because we thought they were larger and a more straightforward shape for all potential gifts from Santa. By the morning the flat white pillowcases were bulging and heavy and we would begin to pull out each of the carefully wrapped gifts, scattering our new possessions across the bed clothes. Nevertheless, the felt Christmas boots that we hang out today do look more attractive and we hope that Santa will take them as welcome decorations.

As I rummaged to the bottom of my own 'stocking' to retrieve the final gift, I always knew it would be a satsuma. The St Nicholas story's most memorable exploit, a consequence of his travels, which has become a popular scene depicted in Christian art, relates a secret gift given to a man who had three daughters.

The man was of lowly means and could not afford a dowry for each daughter, which would have had grave consequences for their marriage prospects. However, St Nicholas heard of the devout man's plight, and knowing he would not want to accept charity publicly or in the daytime, he acted after dark.

On three consecutive nights, he passed by the man's house, throwing a purse of gold coins through an open window, thus saving the daughters from penury or being sold into slavery or prostitution. In some iconography St Nicholas is depicted with three oranges, or other fruit, in a metaphorical reference perhaps to the three purses of gold from this story, and our more modern interpretation of giving oranges or satsumas.

I start my day with a dog walk, as it is best to get this out of the way early. With a cheerful scarf thickly wrapped around my neck and ears, and hands buried into my warm coat pockets, we head down towards the horses' fields. The dogs, noses glued to the frosty grass, scamper off following fresh smells and occasionally rubbing their faces delightedly along the ground into the icy cool crystals. Bella, our most elderly matriarch Labrador, loves nothing better than cooling herself with a thoroughly comprehensive roll. As I check the water troughs are not frozen over, we turn back towards the lodge and the gardens beyond.

The splendid cedars tower over the lawns, their years of growth outliving our generations in magnificent style. The Phoenicians used cedar wood to build their ships, and the Egyptians also used it to construct coffins –

including that of Tutankhamun. Solomon used cedar wood to build Jerusalem and the Romans to make sculptures. It was said to symbolise purification and protection, which might explain why Hebrew priests were ordered by Moses to use the bark to treat leprosy.

The tree is a symbol of Christ: 'His form as of Libanus [Lebanon], excellent as the cedars.' (Canticles 5:15.) The prophet Ezekiel used the cedar as a symbol of the Messiah and His Kingdom. '…I will crop off a tender twig from the top of the branches thereof, and I will plant it on a mountain high and eminent.' (Ezekiel 17:22.) These days, rather more prosaically, Sally uses its scent in one of her handmade soaps in the gift shop.

As the ravens alight, noisily cawing at the top of the tree, I take my leave and call the dogs back to the warmth of the Castle and breakfast.

I heard a bird sing
In the dark of December
A magical thing
And sweet to remember.
We are nearer to Spring
Than we were in September,
I heard a bird sing
In the dark of December.

OLIVER HERFORD

ABOVE
A cedar tree laden with snow

RIGHT
The bridge at Temple Track

FIRST THINGS FIRST
BREAKFAST & OFF TO CHURCH

CHRISTMAS DAY BREAKFAST IS A SPOILING AFFAIR, WITH scrambled eggs and smoked salmon, warming porridge, toast and copious cups of tea and coffee. There is much discussion about what gifts Father Christmas left, how many mince pies he ate, the half-finished glass of whiskey and the carrot tops left behind by the reindeer, as well as have the children been good enough to receive a much-requested toy and what a rush he must have been in to get to his next stop! As a small child, my son Edward would make a list for Santa and pin it to his door. On Christmas morning he would then proceed to carefully tick off what was in his stocking and bring forward what was missing for another year. I could only admire his practicality.

As breakfast finishes, the house party slowly gears up to brave the cold morning air and the Christmas morning church service. It is a truth universally acknowledged that we all, eventually, become more like our mothers! My mother, having such a large number of daughters to rally, would begin the process long ahead of the actual event. One such example would be getting us to church in a timely manner, and so timely was our mother that we would invariably end up in the front few pews, waiting a chilly extra half an hour for the remainder of the congregation to arrive. I'm afraid I am now showing the same propensity and will set off on my own if necessary ... in good time.

Walking along the lane leading to the church, drawn by the peal of bells, I can see cars parked at rakish angles in hedges, hats emerging as familiar figures greet one another with a 'Happy Christmas' and much chatter. The cold air eddying between the churchgoers as they bustle towards the church porch, and the warmth inside. I am neither too early nor too late.

> I heard the bells on Christmas Day
> Their old, familiar carols play,
> And wild and sweet the words repeat
> Of peace on earth, good-will to men!
> HENRY WADSWORTH LONGFELLOW

THE ROTA OF CHURCH FLOWER LADIES HAS DRESSED the church beautifully. Strictly speaking, decorating the church should be done on Christmas Eve, but for the sake of practicality, it has been completed somewhat earlier. Samuel Pepys, the noted diarist, observed that on the first Christmas kept after the Restoration of King Charles II, his pew was decked with the traditional rosemary and bay.

At the beginning of the eighteenth century an article in *The Spectator* described:

> The church, as it is now equipt, looks more like a Greenhouse than a place of Worship: the middle Isle (sic) is a very pretty shady Walk, and the Pews look like so many Arbours of each side of it. The Pulpit itself has such Clusters of Ivy, Holly, and Rosemary about it, that a light Fellow in our Pew took occasion to say, that the Congregation heard the Word out of a Bush, like Moses.

Highclere's church does not resemble a greenhouse but is nevertheless welcoming as the stalwart churchgoers are joined by many more local families, swelling the congregation, who are now happily greeting each other.

The Christmas story begins with an angel, and our church is called St Michael and All Angels. Angels are found across many religions and mythologies, acting as messengers and benevolent beings protecting humans, and also as go-betweens from God to man. Whilst they are supposedly pure spirits, they are frequently ranked in varying ways across different religions. The hierarchies provide rich inspiration for artists, with angels depicted as other-worldly creatures, androgynous in nature with wings, halos and light illuminating the work.

The archangels Gabriel and Michael were popular subjects for Byzantine and European paintings and sculpture. Guido Reni's Michael is luminous,

Guido Reni (1575–1642), *Archangel Michael*, c.1636

standing over the fallen angel Lucifer or Satan, and reinforces the opinion that St Michael was a protector and leader of God's army against the forces of evil. In other Byzantine art he has been depicted with scales to weigh souls on the Day of Judgement.

Our more modest church has no such artwork but was completed in 1870 by the architect George Gilbert Scott to replace the church of 1689 that was on the medieval site next to the Castle. However, some of the monuments from the old church came to St Michael's, including the Jacobean tomb of Richard Kingsmill, and the monument of my husband's ancestor, Robert Sawyer, that dates from 1692.

As we sit expectantly in the pews, waiting for the service to begin, my mind strays a little. I wonder how long the sermon will be, given the tasks ahead after church – I don't want to be late for Chef. Samuel Pepys wrote in 1662 that he had arrived at chapel in Whitehall, London, to hear the sermon upon the song of the Angels and goodwill to all men, 'A poor sermon but too long,' but luckily our vicar's sermon was neither and, after much hearty singing, we return to the Castle.

A MOMENT'S PAUSE
TO REFLECT ON CHRISTMAS PAST

AS THE CHILDREN RUSH THROUGH THE DOORS TOWARDS the Christmas tree, I turn from the front hall into the North Library. In Victorian times there was a large, ancient table in the middle of this part of

the Library, covered with books, with more stacked underneath and comfy chairs next to tables with candelabra. In 1914, however, the Library, and the world, had become a different place. The table was removed because the space was needed as a dining room for wounded soldiers back from the trenches of the First World War, who were recuperating at the Castle.

In August 1914, Almina, the 5th Countess of Carnarvon, transformed Highclere into a war hospital. It was staffed with thirty nurses dressed in raspberry and white uniforms with Dr Marcus 'Johnnie' Johnson on hand day and night. Almina arranged for surgeons such as Robert Jones to come down from London once a week to perform operations in the overhauled Arundel bedroom. Practically situated near the back stairs for discreet and quick access for nurses to come and go without disturbing patients elsewhere in the Castle, Arundel served well as an operating theatre.

The patients who lived in, and those who visited, counted themselves the lucky ones. They were recovering in some sort of paradise, believing optimistically the war would soon be over.

Lady Carnarvon had found her vocation for life and the patients could not thank her enough: she gave them her home and, in the words of soldier and patient John Pollen, 'made it a home for them by personally attending to the many things that make a house a real home … I shall never forget it'.

Just as we went to church, so had the returned soldiers in 1914, but there had been not much talk of a Merry Christmas at that service. It held such a very different, sombre significance from the usual celebratory renditions, with men in khaki filling the pews. They had all sung 'God save the King' and, kneeling during the prayers, the vicar had read out lists of names – the sick, the dead, the wounded, those who served on land or at sea 'For God, For King, For Country'.

Unbeknownst to those at Highclere, their brothers in arms and German opponents called an unofficial truce on Christmas Day 1914 around the battle lines and trenches of Ypres. The impromptu ceasefire appears to have originated as much on the German side of the lines as it had the British, despite both high commands being against any kind of fraternisation. The Germans famously sang 'Stille Nacht', and as the day went on, incremental lines were crossed, barriers broken down and a football match ensued. Of course, the following day the guns resumed their deadly purpose, and the war was very far from over. Another Highclere patient recalls:

> *My dear sister Janet,*
> *I could not sleep before writing to you of the wonderful events …*
> *In truth what happened seemed almost like a fairy tale … clusters of*
> *tiny lights were shining all along the German line … Christmas trees…*
> *and then we heard voices raised in song:* Stille Nacht, Heilige Nacht.
> *When the song finished the men in our trenches applauded … then one*
> *of our own men started singing and we all joined in'. German officers*
> *climbed out and the English went to meet them half way and they all*
> *exchanged gifts. What if our leaders were to offer well wishes in place*
> *of argument, songs instead of slurs, presents instead of reprisals?*
> *Your loving brother*
> *Tom*

LET FEASTING COMMENCE!

Recipes for
ROAST TURKEY
and all the classic
accompaniments begin on
PAGE 210

OUR DAY RESUMES AFTER CHURCH WITH DRINKS IN THE Saloon around the fire, with the children largely resisting the temptation to open any presents. There is, however, careful evaluation of the pile of presents over their size, their interesting shapes or unusual weight, with speculation as to what they might contain. As we are called in to lunch and take our places around the dining table, the delicious smells of turkey and assorted dishes settle the children to the focused business of eating. A feast

is a time when all overeat – there is nothing temperate about Christmas so it is pointless worrying about guilt and diet. It is about eating prowess.

The gleaming Dining Room table can hardly be seen under the piles of crackers, extravagant flowers and silver ornaments, a present in front of each place, immaculate napkins folded in the shape of a Bishop's mitre, a promising collection of glasses laid out as well as salt cellars and dishes full of cranberry sauce.

Christmas traditions vary but table presents have always been an amusing adjunct to the main event in my family. As children growing up, our mother would use table presents as a means of giving her daughters something she knew they would need but that would be far too boring to receive under normal circumstances. Hence socks and pants (the underwear type), gloves and scarves would be wrapped and, once opened, frequently traded between sisters for an improved colour or size. I have, much to my own son's embarrassment, taken much the same tactic, and friends will open their table presents with a degree of hesitation but also, hopefully, a sense of humour.

Table crackers have become an integral part of Christmas Day dining, and our mother would go to great lengths to get the ones that contained numbered whistles, to be played in sequence. Again, I have found myself doing the same and remember one hilarious post-lunch 'concert' where we tooted our whistles in turn to create well-known carols. The secret is to have a suitably robust conductor to rally the orchestra and call the numbers. I'm not sure I recognised any of the carols as they were punctuated with much laughter, and 'No.5' (me) missing her cue rather a lot.

CHOOSE YOUR BIRD

Roast goose might be a traditional dish for Christmas, packed with onions, sage and lemons, but it is not always the first choice of children, so we tend to stick to turkey. This bigger bird has the added advantages of feeding more hungry family and friends and being very versatile for leftovers after Christmas.

WINDING DOWN

ONCE LUNCH HAS BEEN EATEN, CRACKERS PULLED AND toasts made, we abandon the Dining Room – the table covered in paper hats, wrapping paper, empty plates and mostly drunk wine – and retire to my messy study to watch the Queen's Christmas message. This is a tradition that began in 1932 with a radio broadcast by George V. Hugely popular and widely broadcast throughout the world, it was first televised in 1957 with Queen Elizabeth II reading her speech from the Long Library at Sandringham. Her Majesty's message has become, over time, a reflection of our changing history and milestones reached and exceeded.

Supper on Christmas Day involves everyone. The team from the kitchen and banqueting have left to be with their own families, leaving soup in Thermos flasks, and salads and cold meats in the fridge in the kitchens. By 8pm, rather unbelievably, everyone is again thinking about food. Lining up in some sort of queue, we set off into the servery and down the dark, very old flight of stairs into a small hallway, pushing through the first set of doors, then turning right and right again, along the flagstone corridor which leads eventually to the courtyard, the low light encouraging us to hurry.

I look back to check that the gaggle of friends and family are all still following. We go through the kitchen doors again right towards the patisseries where the large walk-in fridge is on my left. The steel shelves are full of carefully labelled dishes – from salads to meats, cold smoked fish, potato salad and plates of cheeses. I start passing out the dishes wondering if we really need take it all, but somehow a chain of ten people balance the dishes and start turning round to make their way back with them. With laughter and delight this next feast is laid on the cloth-covered trestle table at the back of the Dining Room and all the party crowd around, deciding what they cannot resist before finding a place to sit down to chat and eat.

Having found the ability to eat a little more, and even nibble on some cheese, the tasks revert to the relay needed to return dishes to the kitchen, as

ABOVE
Puppies Stella and Freya
hoping for some
Christmas leftovers

well as sharing the washing-up, drying, putting away and setting the breakfast table, after a fashion. Breakfast side plates and cups and saucers are artfully arranged to cover up spillages on the white tablecloths and suddenly it is 9pm and whatever stage it is all at, everyone runs out of the Dining Room.

This is, of course, so that we can indulge in what was the greatest fun – to watch the Christmas episode of *Downton Abbey* at 9pm on television, curled up on the sofa or floor, nibbling a few more favourite treats.

My father used to like to go off to the Harrods food halls to return triumphantly with boxes of crystallised slices of fruits, oranges or figs, which my sisters and I did not really like but tried to because he did. Today, of course, I rather like them as they remind me of him. Watching *Downton Abbey* was surreal and entertaining, the familiar music starting, the Labrador and opening shots and the actors bustling onto the screen and into rooms just around the corner from us. I tended to remember how hot it was when they filmed the Christmas tree scene in July and enjoying listening to Lady Mary singing 'Silent Night'.

The nostalgia and traditions of *Downton Abbey* were the perfect partner for Christmas Day television, coming on after supper, and their absence has left a gap. The fictional story began in Edwardian times but some of our Victorian forebears left the best archive records...

IN MANY WAYS, CHRISTMAS HAS BARELY CHANGED AT Highclere. The 4th Earl recalls in his diary of 1882:

> *The children began their Christmas songs at 7.15 and then followed the receiving and giving of presents, and as yet their spirits and strength have not flagged.*

Christmas dinner was oyster soup, turbot, boiled turkey, roast turkey, roast sirloin of beef, plum pudding, mince pies, trifles and innumerable kinds of dessert. The Earl continues:

> *We have had an unusually happy Christmas ... I have felt stronger than I have felt for a long time and I am very thankful for all the blessings and happiness, which are around me.*

Two days later Lord and Lady Carnarvon's son, Mervyn Robert Howard Molyneux Herbert, was born.

For us, back in the here and now, sharing the same spaces, a memorable day of feasts and treats is over.

CLASSIC ROAST TURKEY
WITH SAGE AND ONION STUFFING

PREPARATION TIME **30 mins**   COOKING TIME **2 hrs 45 mins, plus resting**   SERVES **10–12**

INGREDIENTS

FOR THE STUFFING

40g (1½oz) unsalted butter

1 tbsp olive oil

2 large onions, finely chopped

1 sprig of thyme

200g (7oz) slightly stale
   wholegrain bread, sliced

Zest of 1 lemon

10 sage leaves

2 eggs, lightly beaten

Salt and pepper

FOR THE TURKEY

5kg (11lb) oven-ready turkey

1 bunch of rosemary

1 bunch of thyme

1 bunch of sage

2 strips of pared lemon zest

1 onion, peeled

2 tbsp butter

4 tbsp butter or duck fat,
   melted

METHOD

§   Preheat the oven to 180°C/350°F/Gas mark 4.

§   First make the stuffing. Melt the butter and oil in a large frying pan and cook the onions with the thyme, until they are soft but not browned. Tip into a large bowl to cool and discard the thyme sprig.

§   Meanwhile, in a food processor, blitz the slices of bread with the lemon zest and sage leaves, until you have breadcrumbs. Tip this into the cooled onions and mix it all together. Add a little salt and plenty of freshly ground pepper. Mix, then add the eggs and combine thoroughly.

§   If stuffing the bird, spoon the stuffing mixture into the neck cavity at the base. Secure the skin flap in place with two skewers. If cooking the stuffing separately from the turkey, divide the mixture into twelve balls and set on a baking tray, or pack into an ovenproof dish.

§   Tie all the herbs and lemon zest together in a bunch with some kitchen string.

§   Place the onion and 2 tablespoons of butter inside the turkey's main cavity, then put the bouquet of herbs in the mouth of the main cavity.

§   Truss the turkey legs close together at the foot end and tie tightly with string.

§   Brush the whole of the outside of the turkey with some of the melted butter or duck fat. Put the remaining fat in the base of a large roasting tin.

§   Cover the neck cavity and the feet end of the drumsticks with a layer of foil or baking paper covered in foil. This will prevent them burning and giving the juices that run from the bird a bitter taste.

§   Put the bird in the oven and roast for 2¼ hours. Baste the turkey twice during cooking. Ovens vary – place a strip of foil lightly over the surface of the turkey if you feel the breast skin is becoming too brown.

§   If cooking separate stuffing balls, they need only to be cooked for the last 30 minutes in the same oven as the turkey.

§ Test the turkey to see if it is done: insert a long skewer into the deepest part of the thigh, through into the breast meat. If the juices are clear the meat is done; if they are pink, return the turkey to the oven and cook for another 15 minutes before testing again.

§ Lift the turkey from the roasting tin and place on a platter. Cover with two layers of wide tin foil and leave to rest for up to an hour before carving.

CHESTNUT STUFFING

Horse chestnut trees bear extravagant flowers in the spring and conkers in the autumn, but it is only the sweet chestnut that produces edible fruits. These chestnuts are full of minerals, vitamins and starch, and most important for our ancestors, they can be stored.

Marrons glacés in particular are one way of storing them; they are a delicacy, which are made in the spring after collection and stored to be eaten a further six months later.

Chestnuts are hard to peel so if you use them fresh, score the skin and roast them in the oven for about five minutes, remove and allow to cool. Then you can easily add – indeed crumble – them into the other ingredients.

One end of our turkey is always full of chestnut stuffing.

PREPARATION TIME 10 mins   COOKING TIME 45 mins   SERVES 8

INGREDIENTS

2 tbsp olive oil

3 large shallots
  or 1 large onion, chopped

6 slices streaky unsmoked
  bacon, chopped

1 garlic clove, crushed

200g (7oz) fresh chopped
  chestnuts (or you can buy
  them frozen)

50g (2oz) butter

200g (7oz) fresh
  breadcrumbs
  (blitzed in processor)

400g (14oz) chestnut purée

A good handful of parsley

2 medium eggs

Salt and pepper

METHOD

§   Heat the olive oil in a frying pan and cook the shallots or onion and bacon until soft, which will take around 10 minutes. Add the garlic, chestnuts and butter and cook for another 2–3 minutes. Add all the remaining ingredients, except for the eggs, and mix together. Remove from the heat and season to taste. Mix in the two eggs before you stuff the turkey.

§   If you want to cook some or all of the stuffing separately, spoon into a greased baking dish – 18 × 24cm (7 × 9½ inch) would work perfectlly. When you are ready to cook, heat the oven to 190°C/375°F/Gas mark 5 and bake for 25–30 minutes until crisp on top.

CHRISTMAS GRAVY

PREPARATION TIME **10 mins**   COOKING TIME **30 mins**   SERVES **10–12**

INGREDIENTS

1 tbsp rapeseed oil
1 onion, finely chopped
1 carrot, finely chopped
1 bay leaf
2 tbsp plain flour
1 litre (1¾ pints) homemade
   chicken or turkey stock
Giblets from the turkey
   (but discard the liver)
50ml (2fl oz) white wine
Juices from the turkey
Salt and pepper

METHOD

§   Heat the oil in a frying pan and fry the onion, carrot and bay leaf until the onion is golden, 8–10 minutes.

§   Stir in the flour, then pour in the stock while stirring.

§   Add the giblets and white wine and simmer for 20 minutes.

§   Take the pan off the heat and discard the bay leaf and giblets, then purée the remaining contents of the pan with a hand blender until completely smooth.

§   Take the turkey from the oven and pour the juices from the tin into a jug. Leave to stand so that excess fat from the turkey rises to the top. Skim off as much fat as you can and discard, then pour the turkey juices into the pan with the purée and heat until bubbling, stirring constantly. Season to taste.

BREAD SAUCE

PREPARATION TIME **10 mins**   COOKING TIME **10 mins**   SERVES **8–10**

INGREDIENTS

1 onion, cut in half
6 cloves
600ml (1 pint) full-fat milk
50g (2oz) butter
6 peppercorns
1 bay leaf
3 sprigs of thyme
150g (5oz) white breadcrumbs
60ml (2½fl oz) single cream
Pinch of freshly grated nutmeg
Salt and pepper

METHOD

§   Stud the onion halves with the cloves.

§   Place the milk, butter, onion, peppercorns and herbs into a saucepan. Bring to the boil, then turn off the heat and allow to infuse for 30 minutes. Strain and return the infused liquid to the pan.

§   Add the breadcrumbs and simmer for 3–4 minutes.

§   Stir in the cream. Grate over the nutmeg, add some seasoning, stir well and serve.

§   This can be made in advance and kept in the fridge for up to 3 days.

CRANBERRY SAUCE

PREPARATION TIME **5 mins**   COOKING TIME **10–15 mins**   SERVES **6**

INGREDIENTS

200g (7oz) large cranberries,
   fresh or frozen
100g (3½oz) light brown sugar
80ml (3¼fl oz) ruby port
Zest from 2 clementines

METHOD

§   Place the cranberries, sugar, port and zest into a heavy-based saucepan.

§   Bring to the boil, cover and simmer until the cranberries are soft and just beginning to lose their shape.

§   Serve immediately, or cool and store in sterilised jars (see page 308) for later use.

HIGHCLERE GLAZED CARROTS

These are a delightful accompaniment to Christmas lunch and add some festive colour to the plate.

PREPARATION TIME 10 mins   COOKING TIME 25 mins   SERVES 8–10

INGREDIENTS

500ml (18fl oz) light
   vegetable stock
60g (2½oz) caster sugar
1 star anise
800g (1¾lb) selection of
   baby carrots of various
   colours, peeled

METHOD

§ Bring the stock, sugar and star anise to the boil in a pan. Add the carrots and cook until soft.

§ Remove the carrots, reduce the cooking liquor to a glaze and pour it over the carrots to serve.

BRUSSELS SPROUTS WITH CHESTNUTS

Soggy, tepid Brussels sprouts at school lunches may mean you ignore these delicious vegetables except when occasionally feeling obliged to include them in high days and holidays. In fact they are high in many nutrients, especially fibre, vitamin K and vitamin C. I think they are delicious and in this recipe they are combined with chestnuts. You could also think of chopping them and putting them in a hot wok to stir fry with bacon lardons.

PREPARATION TIME 10 mins   COOKING TIME 8–9 mins   SERVES 8–10

INGREDIENTS

800g (1¾lb) Brussels
   sprouts, trimmed
60g (2½oz) butter
300g (10½oz) cooked,
   peeled chestnuts in a
   vac-pack
4 sprigs of thyme,
   leaves picked
Salt and pepper

METHOD

§ Blanch the Brussels sprouts in a pan of boiling water for 1 minute, then drain.

§ Heat the butter in a large frying pan, add the Brussels sprouts, chestnuts and thyme leaves and season well with salt and pepper.

§ Reduce the heat and cook for 6–7 minutes, stirring frequently, until the Brussels sprouts are cooked through.

SERVING THE CHRISTMAS PUDDING

The serving of the pudding (see page 57 for the recipe) is always a high point of the Christmas celebrations – a moment of drama that everyone remembers year after year from their earliest childhood. Traditionally a sprig of holly decorates the top as a reminder of the Crown of Thorns.

At Highclere, Paul pours over some warmed brandy and sets it alight as he rounds the corner from the servery, bearing it into the Dining Room to general applause. The flames seem to take us back into the realms of folklore with the added fun and superstition of seeking treasure and seeing who will find the lucky coin.

METHOD

§   Remove the pudding from the pantry where you have stored it. Make a pleated foil handle for the bowl so that you can remove it easily from the steamer. Cook it in the steamer for 1½ hours to warm it through properly.

§   When ready to serve, carefully turn the bowl upside down onto a plate and slide off the basin.

§   If you didn't do so when making the pudding, push a few foil-wrapped coins well into the base of the pudding.

§   If you want to set the pudding alight, warm a tablespoon of brandy over a gas cooker flame, or a candle on the Christmas table. At the last moment, tip the spoon towards the flame so that the fumes catch light, and quickly pour the flames over the pudding.

§   Serve with large dollops of brandy butter.

BRANDY BUTTER

One never-forgotten Christmas, my father had made half a pound of brandy butter and it was safely in the fridge. Nanny, however, decided to taste it, and then managed to eat it all. My father was furious – mainly that Nanny was not even sick.

INGREDIENTS

125g (4½oz) unsalted butter (at room temperature)

160g (5½oz) icing sugar, sifted

1 tbsp good brandy

METHOD

§   Work the butter in a large bowl with a wooden spoon until it's light and creamy.

§   Beat in the icing sugar until the butter turns almost white. Then beat in the brandy until well incorporated.

§   Roll the butter into the desired shape and refrigerate until needed.

BOXING DAY

TRADITIONALLY, 26 DECEMBER IS THE FEAST OF St Stephen, the first man to be martyred for believing in Christ and a day for small acts of kindness to others. I always thought Boxing Day was an unexpected name for the day after Christmas, and was relieved to discover it had nothing to do with pugilistic enterprises.

The 'box' is in fact more likely to be a reference to the Christmas box that would have been given as a form of gratuity from a master to his servant. As a servant would be attending his master on Christmas Day itself, so St Stephen's Day, or Boxing Day, would allow staff to return to their families to celebrate with a gift box that might also contain food. Following St Stephen's example of distributing food and charitable aid to those in need, it was also customary for alms boxes to be placed in areas of worship to collect donations for the poor.

Pepys noted in his diary on 19 December 1663 that he contributed to this tradition: 'By coach to my shoe makers and paid all there and gave something to the boys box against Christmas.'

Over the last century, it has become traditional in this country to hold various horse races, most notably the King George VI steeplechase at Kempton Park, along with hunts and football matches, on Boxing Day.

Other, less traditional 'sports' have also emerged, with some brave souls venturing a Boxing Day swim or organising fun runs for charity.

For our part, like other estates, and regardless of the weather, we organise a family shoot; one with plenty of walking to help work off the excesses of Christmas Day. It is a busy and bustling day, which helps disperse any feelings of anti-climax after the Christmas festivities.

THE DAY BEGINS LIKE MANY OTHERS, WITH A WALK outside as the pale winter sun washes the Castle stone with a soft watery light. As I glance at the surrounding cloud, I can only hope the sun persists and holds the rain at bay, but the forecast is somewhat mixed.

Behind the Castle, the stable courtyard is already full of muddy cars, excited dogs and beaters arriving swaddled in layers of hats, coats and boots. Greetings over, they follow the smell of bacon butties which are being carried across to the beaters' room for their breakfast.

Eddie, our head keeper, has lit the fire in there and over a dozen people are sitting on the long wooden benches, steaming hot mugs of tea in hand, and with a colourful collection of scarves and gloves piled high on the table like an impromptu rummage sale. It makes for a timeless image, with those who have lived and worked this land for generations sharing news, anecdotes and tall tales – the room is full of broad accents, long vowels and country common sense.

A SHOOTING PARTY

GEORDIE MAKES HIS WAY OUT OF THE BACK DOOR OF the Castle, avoiding the long-wheel-based cars turning awkwardly to park, to discuss with Eddie which drives he has planned for the day. Those in the room turn to welcome him with large smiles and general calls of 'morning m'lord'.

Both he and the keepers are dressed in hard-wearing Scottish tweed; a traditional cloth that was originally worn by Highland farmers, it became fashionable in the 1820s and 30s. Since then it has fluctuated in and out of fashion – whether promoted as a practical cloth during the war for women to wear as three-piece suits and to cycle in, or given a French twist by Coco Chanel, its durability, versatility and warmth have stood the test of time.

Eddie has gathered about twenty of his team together, all familiar faces: Jane and Ann with their dogs to pick up, along with other longstanding locals and Terry the under keeper and his family, who walk through the woods, spaniels running around without pause, noses to the ground. All of them share a love of the rolling Hampshire countryside, the wooded pasture, the flocks of sheep grazing on turnip stubble, the sound of the birds in the hedgerows and the enthusiasm of the working dogs. It is a good way to spend a day.

Returning with Scooby (one of our Labradors) to the front of the Castle, Geordie is in good time for some coffee and breakfast. Family and friends begin to assemble, collecting cups of coffee and choosing from warmed serving dishes, before finding somewhere to sit down at the immaculate white-clothed table, pots of cyclamen arranged down the centre, jostling with scattered jars of marmalade and honey to smooth generously onto toast. The children clamber onto chairs and then off them, looking for more croissants or scrambled eggs.

Given the short amount of daylight during the winter months, Geordie starts to encourage everyone out and off. Well briefed, well wrapped up and well fed, the guns climb into the waiting vehicles and the motley entourage disappears down the front drive. I turn back into the Castle, carefully close the door behind me and return to the Dining Room. It is my turn for a peaceful cup of coffee with those left behind before catching up with the guns mid-morning. Handily, this also gives me time to confirm numbers and details for lunch and make provision for any extras I might have inadvertently overlooked.

With radio communications a key part of everyday life at Highclere, a shoot can let staff, and most importantly the kitchens, know their movements and where and when they might be expecting to stop for a break, or what time they will be heading back to the Castle for lunch. On discovering that the shooting party are pausing for soup and sausage rolls nearby in the park,

After exertions in the
frosty air, a hearty
lunch is required:
BOXING DAY
BEEF STEW
PAGE 228
...and don't forget
to offer a good
CHEESE BOARD
PAGE 234

I prefer to walk, rather than drive, to meet them and set off with the other left-behind friends and family. Walking at a brisk pace to keep warm, the air fresh and invigorating, we head out across the lawns to cut through Lime Avenue and into 'Wallaces' – a field that conveniently provides a line of trees in the lee of which our shooting party rests, discussing the morning's success. With soup to fortify them, they soon start the walk to the next drive.

The end of the morning comes, and everyone returns to a hearty lunch at the Castle. It is a chance to defrost cold feet and hands and refuel for the shorter afternoon. Given the grey air and hour, and the necessity for a relatively swift lunch break, the kitchens provide food that is simple, wholesome and easy to serve. Pies and casseroles make for nutritious options and are a firm favourite.

Our shooting lunches end with a selection of cheese and quince jelly, which is really an opportunity to pass the port. I have many weaknesses and cheese is one of them, so if there is any leftover following the shoot lunch, it is a perfect excuse to make a cheese soufflé for a quick supper sometime in the next few days.

As etiquette dictates, the port decanter makes its journey clockwise around the table, and those slow to pass it on are nudged. Exactly why it travels left is not clear, but the British Navy lays claim to the tradition, and of course port is left – starboard right. It is also a practical rule for right-handers, as it leaves that hand free to continue to tackle cheese or pudding.

AS THE SHOOTING PARTY RETURN TO THE AFTERNOON'S fading light, and low cloud and mist hangs over Siddown Hill, I gather the dogs, various nephews, nieces, sisters and friends for an afternoon walk before dusk. I am not entirely sure my husband ever thought we would have quite so many dogs, but with plenty of enthusiastic helpers we set off towards the Wood of Goodwill. For the dogs there is something to explore in every shrub and under every tussock of silvered grass. With sticks to retrieve or another dog with which to play tag, their games are endless and happily exhausting.

As we walk under a stepped arch of beech into the Wood of Goodwill, the curling paths open out towards the large expanses of grass, which in spring are dotted with daffodils and crocus. Now, though, the wisps of slim-limbed trees lie bare and dormant and the Six Sister Walk and the clear pattern of the rose arbour are stark silhouettes. We head through the high wooden-slatted gate, counting the dogs through like a school ma'am counting her class off the bus, and continue uphill, the children and dogs running ahead, never short of energy or breath.

All parties return to find tea set in the Saloon, where the broad fireplace and its welcoming fire becomes a focal point upon which to warm cold hands and feet. The tingling sensation of warmth returning to cold cheeks makes the effort of such walks worthwhile and mitigates, in some small way, the excesses of Christmas dining.

THANK-YOU LETTERS

BOXING DAY MOVES US TOWARDS THAT TIME WHEN thank-you letters must be written. My sisters and I used to sit around an old kitchen table in the rattly, windy house above the beach in Cornwall, complaining to our mother that we could not think what to write. Endlessly patient, she would explain that we needed to write what we had done and it should be two pages long. The excitement of our presents waned as we all slowly wrote four or five letters a day until they were all ticked off and posted.

Many were along the same lines: 'Thank you very much indeed for the lovely scarf/drawing pad/toy horse/twister and best of all money. We will enjoy it very much. We had a lovely Christmas by the sea and played football on the beach. Mummy wrote a play for us to act out – it was Cinderella but all the words were backwards and she had written it in the hairdresser's over the last few weeks. She thought it was very funny, so did Nanny.'

From the over-excitement of piles of presents to the diligent letters that are slowly completed, there is a sense of sadness because the companionship and sharing is over for another year. One way to gather oneself together is to go for a walk, to be outside. Another is to cook with warming and stimulating ingredients such as lemongrass and ginger, or even some chilli to pep oneself up. With all those thoughts in mind, a lemongrass broth would be my choice of supper and I would endeavour to acknowledge that some days we simply feel better than others.

The lightest of dishes to refresh after festive excess:
LEMONGRASS AND HERB BROTH
PAGE 226

THE HIGHCLERE CHRISTMAS QUIZ

PART 5

C U L T U R E

1/ Celebrated conductor Sir Malcolm Sargent was a regular visitor to Highclere, but which renowned summer concerts did he conduct from 1948–67?

2/ Henry James visited Highclere and wrote *The Portrait of a Lady* which was adapted as a film starring Nicole Kidman. Which other movie has Nicole Kidman filmed at Highclere?

3/ Dame Nellie Melba, played by Dame Kiri Te Kanawa, performs for Downton Abbey's Lord and Lady Grantham, but can you name the aria she sang, and from which opera and by whom?

4/ What film won the writer of *Downton Abbey* an Oscar?

5/ Can you name two famous authors who came to stay at Highclere?

6/ The Newbury Spring Festival, initiated in 1979 by the 7th Countess, opened with a gala concert including a young performer called Nigel Kennedy. What instrument is he famous for playing, and which famous music school did he attend?

7/ Who composed the theme music for *Downton Abbey*?

8/ Lady Mary and Lady Edith perform to recuperating soldiers at Christmas in *Downton Abbey*, but what song does Lady Mary sing that Matthew joins in with?

9/ There are various Egyptian Clappers exhibited at Highclere, but what was their purpose in Ancient Egyptian culture?

10/ Richard E. Grant made an appearance on *Downton Abbey* as Simon Bricker, but what was the title of his debut film in 1987?

WHO SAID...

11/ 'How scenical! How scenical!' (on travelling through the park to Highclere)?

12/ Above the front door of the Castle is the old French inscription '*Ung je serviray*'. What does this mean?

HIGHCLERE TODAY

13/ How many lodges are there on the Highclere Estate?

14/ How many showers are there within the Castle?

ANSWERS

1/ The Proms 2/ *Eyes Wide Shut* 3/ 'O mio babbino caro', from 'Gianni Schicchi' by Puccini 4/ *Gosford Park* 5/ Henry James; Charles Dodson ('Lewis Carroll') 6/ Violin; Yehudi Menuhin School 7/ John Lunn 8/ 'If You Were The Only Girl in The World' 9/ Instruments to clack together to assist the rebirth of the dead into the afterlife 10/ *Withnail and I* 11/ Benjamin Disraeli 12/ 'One will I serve' 13/ 5 14/ None – there are only baths

LEMONGRASS AND HERB BROTH

After eating too much at Christmas I crave the clean, refreshing taste of lemongrass and I always regard ginger as an important part of my diet, too. Like ginger, lemongrass has health benefits; it reputedly lowers cholesterol, helps with feelings of bloating and to reduce anxiety. I am not sure that I actually feel anxious after Christmas, but the taste of lemongrass is certainly calming.

We are fortunate to have a wide choice of fresh herbs all year round from Highclere's gardens, but you can use whatever you like or have available. All sorts of things can be successfully added to this basic cleansing stock for extra depth and goodness, such as a simple julienne of vegetables or cooked poached chicken breast.

PREPARATION TIME 10 mins   COOKING TIME 30 mins   SERVES 6–8

INGREDIENTS

4 sticks of lemongrass,
   bruised (not chopped)
50g (2oz) root ginger,
   peeled and grated
6 banana shallots,
   finely diced
2 celery stalks,
   peeled and finely diced
4 garlic cloves, crushed
   (without using salt)
20g (¾oz) tarragon
20g (¾oz) oregano
20g (¾oz) rosemary
20g (¾oz) thyme
8 black peppercorns
4 bay leaves
2 tbsp ground turmeric
30ml (1¼fl oz) cider
   vinegar
2 litres (3½ pints)
   vegetable stock
   (it's OK to use a cube!)

METHOD

§   Put all the ingredients into a pan, covering them with the cold stock. Bring everything to the boil, then turn down the heat and simmer for 30 minutes to allow the flavours to infuse the stock. Strain through muslin into a clean pan or bowl and allow to cool a little or enjoy straight away.

BOXING DAY BEEF STEW

Pies and casseroles are hearty and comforting, and are dishes that can be made ahead – the slower-cooked the better. This stew is a firm favourite at Highclere, especially on Boxing Day, providing a contrast to turkey, and served with celeriac mash to soak up the juices.

PREPARATION TIME **15 mins**   COOKING TIME **3 hrs 15 mins**   SERVES **6–8**

INGREDIENTS

2 tbsp rapeseed or
   sunflower oil
30g (1¼oz) butter
1·5kg (3¼lb) lean braising
   steak or similar, cubed
2 large red onions, diced
2 garlic cloves, finely grated
2–3 bay leaves
2–3 sprigs of thyme
2 tbsp plain flour
200g (7oz) chestnut purée
600ml (1 pint) beef stock
1 tbsp redcurrant jelly
A couple of splashes
   of Tabasco sauce
400g (14oz) chestnut,
   shiitake or other
   mushrooms
1 large tbsp plain yoghurt
   or crème fraîche
Salt and pepper

METHOD

§   Preheat the oven to 170°C/325°F/Gas mark 3.

§   Heat the oil and butter in a large casserole dish and season the beef.

§   Add the beef to the pan and seal on all sides. Remove from the pan and set aside.

§   To the same pan add the onions and cook for 5–6 minutes until starting to soften.

§   Return the meat to the pan along with the garlic, bay leaves and thyme.

§   Add the flour and stir to coat everything in the pan.

§   Add the chestnut purée and keep stirring, adding a little of the beef stock to prevent the ingredients catching and burning.

§   Add the redcurrant jelly, Tabasco and some more seasoning, then pour in the rest of the stock, stir well and put into the oven for 2 hours, with a lid on.

§   Remove the casserole from the oven and add the mushrooms. Cook for a further 30–45 minutes, until the meat is tender and breaks apart when pressed with the back of a wooden spoon.

§   Remove the casserole from the oven and stir through the yoghurt or crème fraîche just before serving.

CELERIAC AND HORSERADISH MASH

This is a delicious accompaniment to any red meat dish, especially venison.

PREPARATION TIME **15 mins**   COOKING TIME **25 mins**   SERVES **6**

INGREDIENTS

Juice of ½ lemon

1 celeriac

700g (1½lb) potatoes,
   peeled and cut into cubes

2 garlic cloves, peeled

100ml (3½fl oz)
   full-fat milk

2 bay leaves

2 tsp freshly grated
   horseradish
   (or 2 tbsp prepared
   horseradish sauce)

20g (¾oz) butter

Salt and pepper

METHOD

§   Add the lemon juice to a large saucepan of cold water, to prevent the celeriac turning brown. Peel the celeriac and cut into medium-sized cubes, then put them immediately into the pan of water.

§   Place the potatoes in a separate pan with the whole garlic cloves and cover with cold water.

§   Bring both pans to the boil and simmer for 15–20 minutes until tender.

§   Add the milk and bay leaves to another pan and heat until simmering, then stir in the horseradish. Immediately remove from the heat and let the flavours infuse for 5 minutes.

§   Drain the potatoes, garlic and celeriac, transfer to a large bowl and mash together. Remove the bay leaves, add the warm milk and butter, season to taste and beat with a wooden spoon until smooth.

HOMEMADE LEMON ICE CREAM

Geordie remembers homemade lemon ice cream as a child, a favourite of his mother's as well as his, and neither of them have ever said no to ice cream and sorbets.

PREPARATION TIME 10 mins, plus churning or freezer time   COOKING TIME 10 mins   SERVES 6–8

INGREDIENTS

6 egg yolks
250g (9oz) caster sugar
500ml (18fl oz)
    double cream
200ml (7fl oz)
    single cream
Zest of 2 lemons,
    plus 160ml (½fl oz)
    lemon juice
Seeds of 1 vanilla pod

METHOD

§   Place the egg yolks and sugar into a bowl and whisk together until pale.

§   Put both the creams, lemon zest and vanilla seeds into a saucepan and place over a low heat. Bring everything to a simmer, then turn off the heat and allow to infuse for 15 minutes.

§   Pour the warm cream over the egg and sugar mix in a steady stream, stirring constantly.

§   Allow to cool before stirring in the lemon juice.

§   Transfer to an ice-cream machine for churning and then transfer to a freezerproof container with a lid and store in the freezer.

§   If you don't have an ice-cream machine, this next step can be done by hand in a normal household freezer. You will need to put the ice-cream mix into a freezerproof container with a lid, then transfer it to the freezer for half an hour. Then keep stirring the mixture every 20 minutes to break up the ice crystals over the course of around 4 hours.

BLACKBERRY COMPÔTE

My mother loved compôtes – she would enjoy them at breakfast, lunch or supper. Make far too much of this and use it with porridge, with granola, or serve it as she did, with homemade ice cream.

PREPARATION TIME 5 mins   COOKING TIME 10–15 mins

INGREDIENTS

50ml (2fl oz) water
175g (6oz) caster sugar
1 star anise
1 clove
1 tsp ground ginger
1 tsp ground cinnamon
Seeds of 1 vanilla pod
400g (14oz) blackberries

METHOD

§   Place the water, sugar, star anise, clove, ginger, cinnamon and vanilla seeds into a saucepan and place over a medium heat. Stir gently until the sugar has dissolved, then add the blackberries.

§   Cook for around 5 minutes, longer if you like your fruit more broken down. The berries will start to burst to give you more liquid.

§   When cooked, remove the berries from the heat and allow to cool before transferring to an airtight jar and storing in the fridge.

[CHEF'S TIP: If you blitz this mixture with a stick blender you can make a beautiful puréed coulis.]

Christmas seems to be a time that encourages higher than average cheese consumption in almost everyone. I like to offer a selection of:

Stilton (Colton Bassett or Stichelton), Comté, Cornish Yarg, Cheddar (Montgomery or other), Vacherin (Mont d'Or or Epoisses), Reblochon and Brie (Tunworth or Wigmore).

Alongside, serve a variety of biscuits so that everyone can choose their favourite. I like to make sure we have charcoal biscuits (for soft cheeses), Bath Olivers, Carr's Table Water Biscuits, and some home-made Oat Biscuits (see page 237). And of course our Spiced Beetroot Chutney (see page 33) cuts through all the richness deliciously.

EASY OAT BISCUITS

We grow oats on the farm for both horse feed and human consumption. These crumbly biscuits are perfect with a cup of tea after a long dog walk.

PREPARATION TIME 15 mins   COOKING TIME 20 mins   MAKES 20 biscuits

INGREDIENTS

50g (2oz) caster sugar

100g (3½oz) butter

100g (3½oz) porridge oats (rolled oats, not jumbo oats)

50g (2oz) plain flour, plus extra for dusting

METHOD

§   Preheat the oven to 180°C/350°F/Gas mark 4.

§   Put the sugar and butter into a bowl and cream together with an electric whisk. Add the oats and flour and work them into the mixture well with a wooden spoon. Lightly knead the mixture until smooth and then roll out to a thickness of 5mm (¼ inch) on a lightly floured work surface.

§   Cut into circles using a 6cm (2½ inch) cookie cutter and place onto two greased baking trays.

§   Bake in the oven for 18–20 minutes or until beginning to colour.

§   Remove the biscuits from the oven and carefully lift them onto a wire rack to fully cool.

CHAPTER TEN

FAMILY FUN

❋ MAKING ONE'S OWN ❋ ENTERTAINMENT HARKS BACK TO MY

OWN CHILDHOOD IN CORNWALL, WHERE THERE

was, to begin with, no television. What I love is that, invariably, sociable and amusing grown-ups find themselves playing the most modest of board games and becoming by turns increasingly competitive or laughingly demolished by their junior opposition.

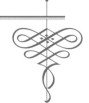

F U N & G A M E S

THERE IS ONLY ONE TELEVISION IN THE ENTIRE CASTLE and it is hidden within a curtained table in my rather untidy study. Furthermore, the puppies have occasionally chewed the controller, rendering it difficult to operate, so we mostly rely on our own resources for entertainment at Christmas.

At Highclere, a particular favourite game of my husband's is 'Sardines'. It seems to have been a much-played game in previous generations, too, and was favoured by Geordie's grandfather. Given the many cupboards, double doors and store rooms here, there is certainly no shortage of hiding places and we find we have to limit the area of play otherwise we would never find one another.

The hider duly disappears, leaving numerous seekers to find him or her. Once found, the successful seeker joins the hiding place as quietly as possible and so on, thus becoming 'sardines' crammed into a virtual tin. Naturally, the choice and size of hiding place can be deliberately small for strategic or amusing reasons – perhaps because the hider wants to remain hidden with a particular seeker!

One year, my husband delightedly found himself in a corner cupboard of one of the bedrooms, joined by various sisters, my girlfriends and other

ABOVE
Playing charades is a
Highclere Christmas tradition

RIGHT
Children playing
hide-and-seek
with Luis and Jorge

240

party guests who'd all managed to find him, and pile into the cupboard. I lost count of quite how many women joined him, but in the end their collective giggles gave them away.

CHARADES ORIGINALLY TOOK THE FORM OF LITERARY riddles, popular in France in the eighteenth century and later adopted by Regency society in England. With clues to each syllable, a cryptic puzzle and a final description of the whole to decipher the word or phrase, they were clever and witty devices to flummox readers of magazines and books or even to flirt and woo a potential suitor. One such charade by William Bellamy reads as follows;

Upon my first I've often sat; my second is a kind of hat;
My whole, a sort of creeping thing that Noah from the ark did bring.

A simpler riddle was included by the 2nd Earl's elder son – later the 3rd Earl – who transformed the family home into the Castle we see today – in a letter, written as a boy; he described it as 'the Queen of riddles':

What colour is the weather?
The storms rose and the winds blew.

Acting charades developed as a parlour game in the early nineteenth century, a variation on the literary, descriptive charades that had been their precursor. With plenty of fictional references in, amongst others, the works of Thackeray and Charlotte Brontë, the popularity of this parlour game endures and is one that is still enjoyed by us all today at Highclere.

Rather than using individuals, we tend to divide the house party into teams, with members randomly pulling cards from a hat to act out a film, book or play. More modern titles have provided rich fodder to both confound and amuse and I clearly remember us laughing so hard we were crying, as Geordie expansively ran up and down the library resorting to acting out the 'whole thing' because his team couldn't make out what he was doing –

the film was *Raiders of the Lost Ark*. My step-daughter Saoirse loves acting out a charade and her enthusiasm can sometimes persuade her brothers to join in.

In December 1883, the 4th Earl wrote proudly in his diary about his eight-year-old daughter Vera (Victoria) and brothers:

> *The children acted Bluebeard ... and extremely well. Vera showed real acting power and was far the best of them all. She spoke distinctly and did not turn her back on the audience ... the little ones Aubrey and Nan looked very pretty dressed up as attendants.*

IN THE SMOKING ROOM WE HAVE MORE TRADITIONAL card tables and a games table that date from about 1770. The fashion for such tables in England during the eighteenth century soon spread as parlour games became de rigueur. Cabinet makers created increasingly elaborate tables, inlaid with marble or delicate marquetry, as well as D-shaped card tables with fold-over tops.

Our games table has a leather-inset top that contains a backgammon board with the reverse being a chess board, and also a game called nine men's morris. This game dates back to the Roman Empire and has been found carved onto Roman buildings and medieval cloister seats in Canterbury, Salisbury and Westminster. Outdoor versions of the game were cut into

ABOVE
An antique games set in the
Smoking Room

village greens and Shakespeare references one such in *A Midsummer Night's Dream* when Titania says 'The nine-men's-morris is filled up with mud'.

It is played on a grid of twenty-four intersections, or points, and players must use their 'nine men' to try to form 'mills', lining up three men either horizontally or vertically, taking turns to place their pieces on the board. If successful at lining three in a row, a player can remove one from the opposition.

Once all pieces are on points, they are then moved from point to point in turn, again with the aim of lining up mills and winning the chance to remove pieces from the opposition. Once either player is down to three pieces, players are permitted to hop or 'fly' from point to point rather than having to move to adjacent points, and the game reaches its natural conclusion.

My mother was a great advocate of card games and taught us to play whist, rummy and bridge. We also spent many a holiday evening playing furiously fast and competitive games of racing demon. My sisters and I are ready to take on any players, although Geordie usually refuses. Racing demon requires quick reflexes, coordination and low cunning and is played at breakneck pace, eliciting frequent shouts of frustration and triumph.

I also rather enjoy playing bridge and, as we have a number of bridge tables in the Library, I always hope that we can find a four amongst us to play a few rubbers. Geordie has endeavoured to learn some of the rudiments but he has memories of his grandfather playing competitively and getting very upset if the cards were not falling to his pleasure so, to provide encouragement, I find the answer is a nice, refreshing, ice-clinking, crystal glass tumbler with gin, tonic and a slice of lemon. It all begins to go much better – and a second restorative glass helps, too! The third definitely doesn't, but by then it is time for supper.

MUMMERS & PANTOMIMES

MUMMERS IS AN OLD-FASHIONED TERM FOR ACTORS who mime a play; the word might come from the old English word 'mum', meaning silent, or the old German word '*mumme*', meaning disguise, but both hold true here.

Traditionally, if mummers are welcomed into a house, they would offer a variety of informal performances that might include dance, music, jokes or recitations. In later centuries they might have a script as well. The hosts had to guess the mummers' identities before offering them food or drink. Once identified, the mummers would remove their disguises, spend some social time with the hosts, then travel on as a group to the next home.

Sweet treats to offer
any passing mummers:
CHRISTMAS
FLAPJACK
PAGE 259
APPLE AND
MINCEMEAT
STRUDEL
PAGE 256

Today we have the pantomime. Designed to suit all ages, with songs, dancing and slapstick, it employs gender-crossing actors and combines topical humour with a story based less, rather than more, on a well-known fairy tale. Sadly, we don't hold one at Highclere but every year Geordie and I go to watch a great friend, the actor Kit Hesketh-Harvey, act in one. We take part, singing along on cue, avoiding the water pistols and shouting out phrases to the performers.

Kit is so entertaining, quite outrageous, and I look forward to it each Christmas. In return he often comes to stay with his cabaret partner, James, and every lunch or dinner is full of impromptu rhymes. We are never so popular with our friends as when they find out he is invited to stay. A firm favourite with all the team at Highclere, I once found Kit in the Dining Room on his knees in front of Diana, our housekeeper. Wondering whether I should retreat, I discovered he was apologising for calling Diana 'Margaret' at breakfast.

One of our team at Highclere, Paul McTaggart, likes nothing better than being part of an amateur dramatic group, having custard pies in his face and dressing up to make the audience laugh. Every year he does a pantomime and every year he practises his lines around the office. He is teetotal but inevitably plays the drunk pirate. It is part of a centuries'-old ritual.

A DAY WELL LIVED

SNOW AND ICE ACCENTUATE THE ARCHITECTURE OF the Castle, but it is the grace and magnificence of the cedar trees that dominate the winter landscape here. In a hoar frost they are almost indescribably beautiful, encrusted with ice crystals.

However cold it has been here recently, it is not nearly as cold as it was in 1683, the year of the Great Freeze, when in London there were parties and carnivals on the frozen River Thames, with people standing on it nibbling gingerbread and sipping glasses of gin. Deep, cold winter revisited Highclere in 1815 and then again 150 years later, when Geordie's father and aunt took to skating on the lake here.

Not trusting the ice on the water in recent snowy days, we have taken instead to sledging on solid ground. Dressed for warmth, those who wish to join in set off with me amidst laughter and expectation. Not everyone who works here lives at Highclere, whether in the park or around the Castle, but often many wish they did and, when it snows, everyone often finds a place to stay amongst the team here. It is safer than driving home, and in some years we have had a lot of snow and ice.

To make the best of the day we abandon our work at lunchtime – it can wait until later – and we take a collection of sledges either to the slopes under the Temple of Diana or those under the Etruscan Temple. In each

OPPOSITE
Sledging at the
Temple of Diana

moment outside, the air is felt more keenly, cheeks turn pink and gloved hands are rubbed together to keep warm.

There is nothing better than sitting on a sledge, feet tucked in, someone giving you a push to start and the crunch of the snow as you bump off down the slope with shrieks and laughter as the sledge and you go the wrong way towards slightly bewildered sheep.

After a while it is possible to ambush those on a sledge with a well-aimed snowball, and of course who does not enjoy snowball fights – my son Eddie leading the way against his brother George.

It is invigorating and unforgettable – such a different feeling compared to the languor of the warmer weather of summertime – and also creates deeper memories. Following any cold winter excursions, the next thing is to go inside for proper hot chocolate and flapjacks or a cup of strong tea with ginger biscuits to dunk.

BROCCOLI AND BLUE CHEESE SOUP

After Christmas, this is a comforting dish made from stock and leftover vegetables and cheese. The salty blue cheese gives a robustness to the broccoli and is inevitably a pretty colour, but do vary the cheese to use whatever you have.

PREPARATION TIME **10 mins**   COOKING TIME **40 mins**   SERVES *6–8*

INGREDIENTS

100g (3½oz)
   unsalted butter

1 large onion, sliced

3 celery stalks, chopped

1 leek (green part only),
   sliced

3 heads broccoli,
   florets and stalks finely
   chopped, separately

200g (7oz) potatoes,
   peeled and diced

1·5 litres (2½ pints)
   vegetable stock

5 garlic cloves, finely sliced

2 bay leaves

300ml (10½fl oz)
   double cream

Salt and pepper

200g (7oz) blue cheese
   (Stilton or Roquefort),
   or more if you wish,
   to serve

METHOD

§   Melt the butter in a heavy-based pan over a medium heat. Add the onion, celery and green part of the leek and sweat for 5 minutes, stirring often until softened but not coloured. Add the broccoli stalks and potato to the pan and cook for 5 more minutes. Now add the vegetable stock, garlic and bay leaves to the pan. Bring to the boil and simmer for 10 minutes.

§   Add the finely chopped broccoli florets and cook for a further 10 minutes.

§   Blitz with a stick blender until completely smooth, then stir in the cream and season to taste. Return to the heat and simmer for a further 10 minutes or until it reaches your preferred thickness. If the soup is too thick, add a little more cream.

§   Just before serving, add the blue cheese and allow it to melt a little.

PRAWN COCKTAIL

Prawn cocktail is back – once again it is one of the most popular hors d'œuvre, having first emerged some forty years ago. It is delicious and can look beautiful in a glass or when constructed carefully on a pretty plate. It is simple and the key is to ensure it is not watery; a baby gem lettuce or chopped avocado is a better choice than iceberg lettuce.

For variety, you could add a tablespoon of brandy to the mayonnaise to give it a twist, or some cucumber (chopped and de-seeded) to the gem lettuce.

PREPARATION TIME 10 mins   SERVES 6

INGREDIENTS

100ml (3½fl oz)
   white wine vinegar
Grated zest and juice
   of 1 lemon
36 peeled raw king prawns
3 baby gem lettuce
60g (2½oz) mayonnaise
60g (2½oz) tomato
   ketchup
1 tsp paprika
1 tsp Worcestershire sauce
Pinch of black pepper
Pinch of cayenne pepper
Brown bread and butter,
   to serve

METHOD

§   Bring a saucepan of water to the boil and add the white wine vinegar and lemon juice. Drop in the raw prawns and cook for around 2 minutes, or until they turn pink and float. Remove, drain on kitchen paper and allow to cool.

§   Prepare the lettuce by removing the outer leaves. Keep the six best leaves and thinly slice the remaining lettuce. Wash in cold water and shake dry.

§   To make the sauce, mix together the mayonnaise, ketchup, lemon zest, paprika and Worcestershire sauce.

§   When you are ready to serve, lay an outer leaf filled with chopped lettuce onto each individual plate, mix the prawns into the sauce and place the prawns on the lettuce with a twist of black pepper and sprinkle with an extra pinch of the cayenne pepper.

§   Serve with brown buttered bread.

ALMINA'S GNOCCHI À LA ROMANA

You may well be familiar with little soft dough-like balls marked with ridges – gnocchi – and made with potatoes. The original Roman gnocchi were made using semolina. This is Almina, the 5th Countess of Carnarvon's recipe from our archives and the gnocchi in this case are flatter, sprinkled with cheese and grilled. Almina's recipe uses Parmesan but you could scatter over a blue cheese such as Dolcelatte or Gorgonzola. Almina suggested serving her gnocchi with a tomato sauce.

This dish makes a delicious starter or a supper dish and just needs a green salad.

PREPARATION TIME 10 mins   COOKING TIME 30 mins   SERVES 6

INGREDIENTS

FOR THE GNOCCHI

1·5 litres (2½ pints) milk
300g (10½oz) semolina
1 tsp grated nutmeg
2 egg yolks
2 tbsp basil, chopped,
    plus extra to serve
2 tsp grated Parmesan
25g (1oz) butter, melted
Salt and pepper

FOR THE SAUCE

2 tbsp olive oil
3 garlic cloves,
    finely chopped
800g (1¾lb) fresh tomatoes,
    finely chopped
    (or two 400g [14oz] tins
    of chopped tomatoes)

METHOD

§   First make the gnocchi. Bring the milk to the boil and scatter in the semolina, nutmeg and some seasoning, whisking constantly. You may need to add a little more milk if it gets too thick too quickly.

§   Cook gently, stirring occasionally, for 15–20 minutes until smooth and thick enough to stand the spoon up in.

§   Remove from the heat and beat in the egg yolks and chopped basil.

§   Spread the mixture into a lightly-oiled tray, about 1·5cm (½ inch) deep. Allow to cool a little, then chill for a minimum of 4 hours in the fridge.

§   Once cold, cut into 2·5cm (1 inch) cubes and layer into a buttered ovenproof dish.

§   Sprinkle with grated cheese and melted butter and brown the top under a hot grill.

§   While the gnocchi are grilling, make the sauce. Heat the oil in a large pan over a low heat and fry the garlic for a minute.

§   Add the tomatoes and season generously. Cook for 10 minutes until slightly reduced and thickened.

§   Serve the gnocchi with the sauce and the basil leaves scattered over.

MACARONI CHEESE

My mother loved macaroni cheese, particularly the crisp cheesy top, and it was an easy supper dish in the holidays when there were so many of us and the cooking and planning never ceased. This is best served simply with a green salad.

PREPARATION TIME **30 mins**   COOKING TIME **20 mins**   SERVES **6**

INGREDIENTS

700g (1½lb) dried macaroni

50g (2oz) unsalted butter

50g (2oz) plain flour

1 litre (1¾ pints) full-fat milk

200g (7oz) grated cheese (Black Bomber, Gruyère or mature Cheddar)

English mustard, to taste

Herbs (chives, tarragon and rosemary all work well), to taste

Salt and white pepper

METHOD

§   Preheat the oven to 200°C/400°F/Gas mark 6.

§   Cook the pasta in a pan of boiling salted water until al dente (this means until just undercooked, with a little bite – reduce the stated cooking time by around 2 minutes). Drain the pasta in a colander and cool under cold running water. Drain and shake dry, then set aside.

§   Now, for the sauce, melt the butter in a heavy-based pan over a medium heat.

§   Add the flour to the butter and 'cook out' the flour without letting it get too much colour – you are looking for a sand colour – until it forms a roux; this will take a couple of minutes.

§   In a separate pan, bring the milk to a simmer.

§   Now incorporate the warmed milk into the roux, working it in one ladle at a time and stirring each addition with a wooden spoon to make a smooth white sauce.

§   Add the cheese, mustard, herbs and stir well. Taste and add salt and white pepper, if desired. Tip the cooked pasta into the sauce and stir to coat.

§   You now have a rich macaroni cheese ready to be placed in an ovenproof dish and baked for 20 minutes, or until golden and bubbling.

[CHEF'S TIP: This is such a great comfort food and also a dish that you can add almost anything to, such as garlic, ham, peas, roasted pine kernels, smoked salmon and a multitude of herbs.]

PHEASANT IN CIDER

This is a great winter warmer which we often serve to our beaters during the shoot season.

PREPARATION TIME **15 mins**   COOKING TIME **40 mins**   SERVES **4**

INGREDIENTS

4 pheasant breasts,
  skin removed

30g (1¼oz) unsalted butter

4 rashers smoked streaky
  bacon

2 apples, skin on, cored
  and cut into wedges

500ml (18fl oz) good
  English cider

2–4 shallots, finely chopped

30g (1oz) plain flour

100ml (3½fl oz)
  full-fat crème fraîche

Salt and pepper

Rosemary sprigs

Kale and potato or celeriac
  mash (see page 230),
  to serve

METHOD

§   Preheat the oven to 160°C/310°C/Gas mark 3.

§   Rub the pheasant breasts all over with a little of the butter.

§   Using a rolling pin, roll the bacon between two pieces of greaseproof paper to thin it out, then wrap each pheasant breast in a rasher of bacon.

§   Place a large ovenproof dish on the hob over a high heat and add the breasts, along with the apple wedges for around 5 minutes, turning until the bacon has started to take on some colour. Add half the cider then transfer to the oven to roast for 30 minutes. Put the rest of the cider into a small saucepan and cook until reduced by half.

§   Cook the shallots gently in the rest of the butter until soft and starting to caramelise. Stir in the flour, and then little by little add the cider reduction and cook over a low heat until the sauce starts to thicken. Stir in the crème fraîche and continue stirring until it is completely heated through. Season to taste with salt and pepper. (You can always add some more of the cider from the pheasant if you like.)

§   Remove the pheasant from the oven and serve alongside the sauce. Finish with a final twist of black pepper and garnish with rosemary.

§   Serve with kale and mash to soak up the delicious juices; either mashed potato or a celeriac mash work really well.

APPLE AND MINCEMEAT STRUDEL

This is a lovely warming pudding, which is lighter than Christmas pudding but still evokes that festive flavour of spices and mincemeat.

PREPARATION TIME **25 mins**   COOKING TIME **45 mins, plus cooling**   SERVES **8–10**

INGREDIENTS

3 cooking apples (Bramleys are best), peeled and thinly sliced

1 heaped tbsp soft brown sugar

225g (8oz) mincemeat (homemade or from a good-quality jar)

Grated zest of 1 orange

Grated zest of 1 lemon

½ level tsp mixed spice

½ level tsp ground cinnamon

50g (2oz) flaked almonds

25g (1oz) white breadcrumbs

50g (2oz) unsalted butter

4 sheets filo or strudel pastry (there are some excellent frozen, ready-made brands)

Icing sugar, for dusting

Ice cream or whipped cream, to serve

METHOD

§   Preheat the oven to 190°C/375°F/Gas mark 5.

§   Put the apples in a large bowl, sprinkle over the sugar and stir. Add the mincemeat, orange and lemon zests and spices and mix thoroughly.

§   In another bowl combine the almonds and breadcrumbs.

§   Melt the butter.

§   Line a baking sheet with greaseproof paper, arrange the first sheet of pastry over it, and brush with melted butter, then sprinkle one-third of the almond and breadcrumb mixture all over.

§   Put the second sheet directly over the first and repeat. Then do the same with the third sheet, brushing it with butter and scattering with the remaining almonds and breadcrumbs.

§   Put the last sheet of pastry on top, brush with butter, and place the apple and mincemeat filling all along the pastry, leaving a gap of about 5cm (2 inches) around the edge. Now roll up into a sausage shape, tucking in the ends as you go and turn the strudel over so that the pastry seam is underneath.

§   Brush the whole surface with the remaining butter and bake in the centre of the oven for 40–45 minutes.

§   Let the strudel cool for 15 minutes, then dust it with icing sugar and serve with ice cream or whipped cream.

CHRISTMAS FLAPJACK

I think this was one of the first biscuits I used to make as a child with my sister Sarah and we were very proud of them. In fact, we would probably use up all the oats and take everything we made into school. They were just butter, syrup and oats really but the reason it was called a flapjack is not at all clear.

Shakespeare referred to them in *Pericles* (Act II Scene I):

Come, thou shal't go home, and we'll have flesh for holidays, fish for fasting-days, and moreo'er puddings and flap-jacks, and thou shalt be welcome.

This is a lovely recipe for Christmas, which adds some cranberries and orange zest as a delicious variation. Best made with the help of children.

PREPARATION TIME **5 mins, plus soaking**   COOKING TIME **15 mins, plus cooling**   MAKES **16+**

INGREDIENTS

150g (5oz) dried cranberries
350g (12oz) butter
250g (9oz) golden syrup
250g (9oz) demerara sugar
550g (1¼lb) rolled oats
Pinch of salt
Zest of 1 orange

METHOD

§   Preheat the oven to 180°C/350°F/Gas mark 4.

§   Soak the cranberries in water for 5–10 minutes to soften, then drain.

§   Melt the butter and syrup together in a pan. Add all the remaining ingredients and mix well.

§   Press firmly into a greased and lined 25 × 35cm (10 × 14 inch) baking tin. Bake for 10–15 minutes, leave to cool slightly before turning out, and cut into portions when cool.

CHAPTER ELEVEN

THE TWELVE DAYS OF CHRISTMAS

ON THE FIRST DAY OF CHRISTMAS MY TRUE LOVE GAVE TO ME

A partridge in a pear tree
Two turtle doves
Three French hens
Four calling birds
Five gold rings
Six geese a-laying

Seven swans a-swimming
Eight maids a-milking
Nine ladies dancing
Ten lords a-leaping
Eleven pipers piping
Twelve drummers drumming

IN TODAY'S WORLD WE TEND TO ANTICIPATE THE MAGIC OF CHRISTMAS, WITH CHRISTMAS DAY AS THE culmination of the festivities. In the past, though, Christmas Day was just the beginning of the Twelve Days of Christmas, brought to a close instead by the parties and feasts of Twelfth Night, or Epiphany, on 6 January.

A colourful salad to revive you after the heaviness that can attend much Christmas feasting:

PEAR, ROQUEFORT AND WALNUT SALAD

PAGE 276

ON THAT DAY OF EATING AND DRINKING, ROLES IN society were traditionally reversed, with the servants – the 'downstairs' – being served by the masters – the 'upstairs'. This tradition dates back to Medieval and Tudor times when Twelfth Night marked the end of the twelve-day reign of the Lord of Misrule. It also marked the official end of 'winter', which had started on 31 October with All Hallows' Eve (Halloween).

The old English carol 'The Twelve Days of Christmas' reminds us of the story. It is both a feat of memory and perhaps also of arithmetic as, if you keep multiplying the number of presents, by the time you reach the night before 6 January, Epiphany, your true love will have given you a total of 364 gifts.

After Boxing Day, the church celebrates the Feast of St John, apostle and evangelist. Born in Bethsaida, he was called to follow Jesus while mending his nets, and many of his words and letters still subconsciously inform our life today:

> *He that loveth his brother abideth in the light, and there is*
> *none occasion of stumbling in him.*
> 1 JOHN 2:10

The most treasured possessions are friends, and they will support you. The family and friends who were invited for Christmas now leave and, for all the pleasure and goodwill they brought with them, we are very grateful for a few days on our own, to walk, to enjoy some winter soups and colourful salads and a few companionable silences. Whilst Highclere needs to embrace the world of marketing, PR and social media, I certainly need some time to find the other essential side of life: a space to stand and stare, otherwise we have no time to see...

> *Where squirrels hide their nuts in grass.*
> *No time to see, in broad daylight,*
> *Streams full of stars, like skies at night ...*
> *... A poor life this if, full of care,*
> *We have no time to stand and stare.*
> WILLIAM HENRY DAVIES, *LEISURE* (1911)

Walking towards the Chapel and its graveyard, which lie a mile north and downhill from the Castle, the dogs run around inspecting the gardens of the group of cottages built at various points over the last one hundred to three hundred years. Originally, these cottages provided accommodation for the staff who worked in the huge kitchen garden, the orchards, the milking yard, the piggery and chicken runs. Then, during the Second World War, this became an even busier part of the estate when they were lived in by land girls dedicated to helping the 'Dig for Victory' campaign.

LEFT
The Temple of Diana, another of the Highclere Estate follies

Over the last few years we have gradually begun to renovate them. When I first came to live here, I remained entirely muddled as they were called Dairy Farmhouse, Dairy Cottage (bigger than the Farmhouse), Dairy Bungalow, Dairy Cottage 1, Dairy Cottage 2, Dairy Cottage 3 and The Dairy. In order for my project management not to become even more challenged because I would not know which building I was talking about, I have also slowly begun to rename as well as renovate them and now they have a new life as cosy homes for friends.

Behind the cottages are the remains of some old greenhouses, and leaving the dogs trapped outside beyond the metal gate, we walk into where the chickens live. The hens are always keen to see us in winter and lead us towards the old brick building which houses the bins full of their feed and grain. With any luck, there will be the occasional egg from one of them at this time as they begin to register the slowly increasing length of days. We even have some Marans (French hens, just as in the carol) from the south-west region of France. They lay extremely dark brown eggs, though not always regularly.

To one side of the chickens is a faded and patched brick wall topped with capping stones which are no longer quite perfect. An archway reveals the sloping expanse of the old kitchen garden, and at the very bottom, nearly out of view, is another door leading to an orchard of ancient apple and pear trees – almost undoubtedly with partridges in them.

Before the advent of supermarkets, this would have been a hive of activity, producing all the vegetables and fruits required by the Estate. Above the arched entrance the date 1771 is inscribed. Part of renowned landscape architect Capability Brown's grand plan for Highclere for Geordie's ancestor, the sloping land represents thousands of tons of soil cleared and re-shaped to face south and west. No longer used as a vegetable garden, it has become a sort of Secret Garden and, like every walled garden, spurs unconscious memories and stories.

Capability Brown conceived this walled working garden as an arcadia whose first myth began with the Garden of Eden. In fact, the word paradise comes from an old Persian word meaning enclosed garden. Pastoral places and gardens are embedded in the dreams and culture of much of this country – from Shakespeare's blessed plot, 'this earth this realm' onwards – and as I stand here I can imagine the past glories of this working space and conjure promises of future plans which may or may not ever come to fruition.

Behind an adjacent wall live our two new additions: Thelma and Louise, two British Lop pigs. They live in a fenced area of semi-woodland, which was land that had been derelict since the 1950s. Rather than use farm machinery or constantly fighting by hand to improve it, we bought two pigs.

LEFT
Lady Carnarvon feeds her chickens in the old greenhouses

BELOW
The Herb Garden under a blanket of snow

BELOW
Lady Carnarvon tends to the
pigs – two British Lop sows
named Thelma and Louise

RIGHT
View across the Highclere
Estate on a frosty winter's
morning

To begin with it looked a Herculean task even for them, but within the first four months, the transformation was extraordinary. They effectively till the soil. British Lop pigs are an old endangered breed but one that can live outside, are very friendly and just need a bit of sun protection and somewhere to wallow. They love a scratch behind their ears, along their back or in their elbow and will almost collapse in happiness, although I would rather not catch my foot or leg underneath their contented sides.

The soil, now it has been rootled around in, no longer looks compacted and it is easy to see how useful pigs have been to us over the millennia. From a holistic perspective this might be how they used to farm here in past years, although it may well have been more intensive during the years of the Second World War when the alleged 'Arcadian romance' of earlier centuries was finally overturned in the brute survival of the conflict. It changed the purpose of the countryside – every acre had to provide food.

The concrete remains of what were perhaps barns for pigs testify to the number that must have been reared every year. With a surfeit of food and shopping today, the circumstances are different from those of my parents and grandparents.

UNCERTAIN TIMES

ECHOING THE ASSUMPTIONS OF THE FIRST WORLD WAR, in the autumn of 1939 everyone hoped that the war would be over by Christmas. It wasn't, and over the following six years the familiar Christmas traditions and meals had to change. It became a time of year that highlighted the separation of family and friends, children billeted away in the countryside from parents living in the towns, women called up to work in factories and both sexes serving abroad.

Smith, the Highclere Butler, was too infirm to be called up and most evenings could be found listening to the wireless set in his sitting room at the back of the Castle, the clipped voices delivering the news whilst, at Christmas, he also much enjoyed the carols. He had been to church on Christmas Eve but it was strangely silent, no happy peal of bells as they would have been the signal for an invasion.

On the first Christmas of the war, George VI gave a special live broadcast which concluded with words of encouragement from a poem by a British poet Minnie Haskins. It was instantly immensely popular.

Fifty nursery school children from Willesden, north London, mostly three- to four-year-olds, had been evacuated to Highclere in September 1939 and spent Christmas in the huge blacked-out Castle, huddled up at

THE GATE
OF THE YEAR

And I said to the man
who stood at the gate
of the year:
'Give me a light
that I may tread safely
into the unknown.'
And he replied:
'Go out into the darkness
and put your hand into
the Hand of God.
That shall be to you
better than light and
safer than a known way.'

MINNIE HASKINS

HUMBLE PIE

One of Nanny's oft-used phrases was to remind us 'to eat Humble Pie', by which she meant we should apologise for a serious mistake. Humble pie is also a term for a variety of pastries based on medieval meat pies. The word 'humble' in this context comes from the Middle English umbles, or the edible offal, and it thus involves chicken liver, other offal, good dark beer, vegetables, herbs, cinnamon and a pastry topping.

night in the dormitories created for them on the top floor. There was a Christmas tree in the Library and the teenagers, Henry (later the 7th Earl of Carnarvon), his sister Penelope and cousin Patricia, returned home for some of the school holidays, sang carols and found the children small presents. Father Christmas was doing his best, but he was having a few troubles getting through.

In 1940, the British government, anticipating food shortages, began rationing. Lord Woolton was appointed Minister for Food, remaining in that position for the entirety of the war. Known in the press as Uncle Fred, and perceived as a rather avuncular Father Christmas figure, he advocated a simpler diet. As butter, bacon, sugar and meat were all rationed, recipes such as the Woolton Pie, which consisted of carrots, turnips, parsnips and potatoes in oatmeal with a pastry or potato crust, were invented. There were no ration coupons required for fruits or vegetables and the kitchen garden in 1939 would have been full of potatoes, swedes, turnips and greens. Eggs, amongst other foods, were subsidised to keep prices affordable but were freely available if you had your own hens.

Given the school children living at Highclere, the milk from the dairy herd was retained. They all looked forward to a walk down to the dairy, with its huge churns and unique milky smell. They might get a glass of warm foamy milk and later even some cheese, but there were no fancy French cheeses for anyone at Highclere for the next few years. Dairy still plays a role in cooking in my family, whether as butter or cream or making a rice pudding for a winter's evening. The latter is a traditional dish in many countries of the world, and one so simply made, slowly cooking in the oven, then enjoyed with a dollop of jam.

Gifts and decorations were discouraged unless homemade. The children helped their teachers and nurses make paper chains and paint them red and blue. Christmas wrapping paper became scarcer and scarcer, which meant that either people had to be extremely inventive or presents were less of a surprise.

Everyone carefully tried to make the best use of their coupons, and life revolved around the yellow, green and blue books. Restrictions and shortages soon took their toll as a Christmas cake may still have smelt wonderful but it was without raisins and sultanas and possibly several other ingredients as well.

Yet what was most treasured was a postcard, a Christmas card, a line or a letter from a beloved family member or friend, the paper flimsy but the thoughts and words far from it. In December 1942, King George VI spoke of those who had lost loved ones or been parted from them and of his and the Queen's feelings of sorrow, comfort, but also pride.

Today, despite the prevalence of emails, thank-you letters appear over the next few days to be read with a cup of coffee and are a treasured record to keep for both our memories and those of our successors.

OPPOSITE
The Christmas turkey carcass and vegetables simmering in the stockpot

L E F T O V E R S

DURING CHRISTMAS WE ALL DRAW ON MEMORIES OR moments of childhood, just as our own children and grandchildren will. My childhood memories of lunches and suppers in the days following Christmas were of my mother planning how to use the leftovers. We often spent Christmas in Cornwall by the sea, where the extended festive period meant everybody had a holiday, so local shops would be closed. My mother's enterprising ways with ingredients to make food go further were very much a feature of family meals.

Even if the choice of food in the supermarkets around Highclere is not in short supply, I too very much enjoy the challenge of turning leftovers into delicious meals and ensuring that we make the most of everything.

If we set off on a walk, weather being equal, is there anything better than stopping in the shelter of an old slate mossed wall to sit and eat a sandwich made of fresh bread full of turkey, watercress, cranberry sauce and mayonnaise.

Leftover meats can be used just as cold cuts, turned into mince, a curry, a gratin or rissoles. Brussels sprouts can be roughly chopped and roasted in a little oil with pancetta and added to roasted fennel or a salad. Leftover carrots can be reheated and sautéed with a little honey and freshly grated

A noble way to use up the inevitable leftover turkey:
TURKEY RISSOLES WITH TOMATO SALSA
PAGE 282

ginger, and who doesn't love colcannon or bubble and squeak?

The turkey bones all go into the largest saucepan to make a delicious stock. Cover the bones with water and throw in an assortment of vegetables such as leeks, celery and carrots, plus black peppercorns and a handful of herbs, and simmer for an hour or so. Strained, cooled and put in the fridge, the stock becomes the essence of many a good soup.

My father used to love Christmas pudding pan-fried in butter with the remaining brandy butter and the inevitable Cornish clotted cream – rather richly indulgent 'fuel' for leading us on windy, rainy walks across empty beaches or beside vertiginous clifftops.

NEW YEAR'S EVE
'FOR THE SAKE OF AULD LANG SYNE'

OF COURSE, IN SOME WAYS, NEW YEAR'S EVE IS JUST another day, but it should also be, and is, one of reflection, of putting last year to bed and metaphorically tidying the accounts before stepping forwards into the New Year. Tradition and superstition become very intertwined as 'you could open the back door to let the new one in the front door'.

My parents were not particularly bothered by it and often did not even stay up to see the New Year in, which, as children, we always found most disappointing. As we grew older, we were allowed to stay up until midnight and we felt very important. Today, however, other family members and friends have stronger views concerning the importance of an event, so we celebrate with a party and a variety of entertainment.

By heritage, my sisters and I are partly Scottish, thus Highclere now incorporates a few traditions from north of the border. Hogmanay in Scotland is as big a celebration as Christmas is in the south. Looking back to the sixteenth century, when the Protestant reformation looked so sternly upon any celebrations of Christmas, New Year in Scotland became the alternative time to make merry. The old year was burned out with fires, eating and drinking and a ceremony called first footing.

At midnight the first footer knocks on the front door carrying a lump of coal, some salt, mistletoe and sometimes some money. With not a word being said, he enters the house, puts the coal on the fire, the mistletoe on the mantelshelf and the money and salt on the table. Only then does he wish everyone Happy New Year before being welcomed and given a drink. Everyone then shares a cake – a black bun.

Given the weather is often inclement, most of my guests for New Year's occasions live nearby. The form of the evening that seems to work very well at Highclere is for guests to arrive at 8pm, although I am always downstairs in the front hall much earlier to meet the bagpiper and check the

OPPOSITE
Fireworks light up
the night sky

floodlights are turned on outside the Castle. Dressed in immaculate white spats, swinging kilt, a bearskin of a hat and a warm jacket, we begin the evening outside welcoming guests with the haunting sounds of the lone piper. The music floats around the shuttered bedrooms and guests arrive with a sense of ceremony in a deep winter night. There is, however, no rest between notes, nor can the volume be changed, so there is the added advantage that, if the piper begins outside, there is the chance that the smaller children staying in the house might doze off before the evening really gets going.

Family hurry down the stairs, and guests, parking in front of the Castle, scurry into the warm. As they pass through the tall inner doors into the Saloon, it dawns on them that they have the prospect of Scottish reeling, a fact I sometimes obscure to the more retiring of my friends. It is now too late to escape, despite some desperate side glances, but champagne and cocktails soon bring smiles and conversation.

As soon as we have a quorum, I have the music (a sound system) at the ready. The piper stops and comes in for a rest and a wee dram and we are off. The first reel is inevitably the Dashing White Sergeant, in which guests have to line up in groups of three. Brushing aside English reserve, I stand people together and ask them not to move. We walk it through and then there is the wonderful moment as the music begins with a roll. Fortunately, with a few experts amongst the assembled gathering, those less well-versed soon pick it up. In fact, it is the most enormous fun and no-one is left out, whatever their age.

My mother-in-law is on her feet for the Dashing White Sergeant, then joins the others sitting out to watch as the more energetic dances proceed. The Saloon is the perfect size for four eightsomes or one long line for reels that need to go the length of the room. I catch Luis and Charlotte to make up the numbers but Jorge has run downstairs to help Chef and Matthew has run upstairs ...

On one evening, Sally, in charge of one eightsome, was so busy teaching that she lost time during the 'teapots', which was very funny and a few steps later they seemed to be doing it all in double-quick time in a wild effort to catch up. (A teapot is when the man places his right arm round his partner's waist, the lady her left arm round his waist, and all the ladies place their right hand in the middle of the set, joining hands with the other ladies and all round clockwise.)

Later, dancing the Reel of the 51st with my friend Tom, I was delighted, despite his best efforts to spin me round at an ever greater rate, that he was more out of breath than me, given he is training for the London Marathon. That particular reel always begins with order and descends into a mass of introductions, some correct and some not.

Revived, the bagpiper has returned, and as the hour approaches 9.30pm, he kindly pipes us into dinner. The Dining Room has been set out with four round tables, cosy for conversation and comfortable for the room. It is a dinner without hurry, one to breathe in and savour a little wine, to try each new one with each course.

Amazingly, the evening has passed by already and it is time to gather together, ready with a glass of champagne to look forward to a New Year, and then to stand in a circle and sing 'Auld Lang Syne' and wish each other peace and prosperity.

NEW YEAR'S DAY
ON BEACON HILL

LIME AVENUE ALIGNS ON A NEAR NORTH-SOUTH AXIS, some five hundred yards from the Castle, and follows an organised line. It was probably planted in the eighteenth century when there was hope that man was a rational being and that there was a plan and purpose to life. At the top the path divides and one spur takes a cutting through towards Beacon Hill. Out of the trees, the steep escarpment comes into view where the side banks have been chamfered and worn by man's endeavours over thousands of years. At the top I can just see the outline of the rim of the fort.

If we are riding, we take the horses to the far side as they can cover the ground far more quickly. This also avoids slipping on a steep slope. By foot it is a steep climb up the east side, but in either case it is the best way to begin a New Year. Clambering up to the skyline, we stop to take in the views of the broad landscape, a 360-degree panorama. Like others in England, the fort would have been hewn and built some 3,500 years ago, a protective enclosure in the middle of a settled farming community.

The Wayfarer's Walk runs just south of here, going westwards towards the old sacred landscapes of Wiltshire with its henges, circles, tumuli and long barrows. We have burial mounds here, too, and the remnants of

ABOVE
View of Highclere Castle from
Beacon Hill

273

trackways that linked these places together. Walking through the opening into the centre of the fort, there is a deep intuitive sense of time.

Of course, Geordie's great-grandfather, of Tutankhamun fame, is also buried up here. He spent sixteen years excavating in craggy, desolate valleys in Egypt, finding evidence of life, feasts, magic and traditions from antiquity. On his death he found his place to rest in this ancient wild place. Standing by a stone beacon on our New Year's Day, the views lead me to imagine how people lived and stood here, worshipping and shaping their landscape so many centuries before.

> *And then there is also a need that each should understand where he came from and what he is—and what will become of him.*
> WULFSTAN, ARCHBISHOP OF YORK (1002-23)

For all the centuries, for all the millennia that have passed, we all need rituals and ceremonies to give meaning to our lives.

We return, light of step, down the hill to warm fires and a delicious lunch to wish each other well as our last guests depart and a new year begins.

Serve something spectacular
to see in the New Year:

BEEF FILLET
WELLINGTON
PAGE 284

POACHED PEARS
IN RED WINE
PAGE 286

THE HIGHCLERE CHRISTMAS QUIZ
PART 6

IN THE KITCHEN

1/ Dame Nellie Melba visited Downton Abbey, and had a pudding created in her honour. Can you name three key ingredients to her pudding?

2/ People have been eating ice cream for centuries. What ice cream 'accessory' was first created in 1903?

3/ During the First World War, food shortages led to the introduction of ration cards in 1918. Can you name three specific food items that were rationed?

4/ Auguste Escoffier famously supervised the kitchens of the Savoy, and was called upon by Almina to cater for the Prince of Wales when he came to stay at Highclere. What five French 'mother sauces' did he refine and promote as fundamental to French Cuisine?

5/ Highclere is a shooting estate, and game is an integral part of today's menus. What is traditionally the first date of the UK pheasant shooting calendar?

6/ The Wood of Goodwill includes a 'Six Sisters Walk' — an avenue of nut trees. Which nut?

7/ Downton Abbey's cook Mrs Patmore once said; 'Talk about making a silk purse out of a sow's ear. I wish I had a sow's ear, it would be better than this brisket.' What cut of meat is brisket?

8/ The Victorian Still Room would have been used to what purpose?

9/ The Orangery was a fashionable addition to wealthy residences from the seventeenth century onwards, to cultivate delicate or imported plants, such as pineapple and citrus trees. Citrus fruits provide which vitamin especially?

10/ Cream teas are a particular favourite in the Highclere tea rooms, but debate is fierce as to which comes first, cream or jam. Which two counties dispute the cream/jam order, and which way round do they do it?

HIGHCLERE TODAY

11/ Highclere has two lodges that offer exclusive, occasional accommodation. Can you name them?

12/ How many mince pies are consumed at Highclere over the Christmas period?

ANSWERS

1/ Peaches, vanilla ice cream, raspberry sauce 2/ The ice cream cone 3/ Sugar; meat; butter; margarine; cheese 4/ Béchamel; Velouté; Espagnole; Hollandaise; Tomate 5/ 1 October 6/ Walnut 7/ From the breast or lower chest of beef or veal 8/ For making jams, preserves and jellies; and for making tea, coffee and hot chocolate 9/ Vitamin C 10/ Devon: cream then jam; Cornwall: jam then cream 11/ Grotto Lodge and London Lodge 12/ 4,500

PEAR, ROQUEFORT AND WALNUT SALAD

When my parents-in-law came to supper in the cottage that Geordie and I shared before we moved into Highclere, Geordie would start hassling me well before: had I done this? ... had I done that? ... no garlic, no uncooked onions, etc. One of my favourite starters was this straightforward salad.

My father-in-law was originally taught to make this salad by his beloved French governess Mademoiselle Huc, known as 'Doll' to all the family. It could not be simpler, and I could prepare it ahead which meant I was ready at 8pm. Although it is delicious on its own, this salad also lends itself brilliantly to game birds such as pigeon or pheasants.

PREPARATION TIME **20 mins**   SERVES **6**

INGREDIENTS

FOR THE SALAD

3 medium ripe pears
   (Conference or William),
   peeled, cored and sliced
150g (5oz) Roquefort
   cheese, crumbled
120g (4¼oz) walnut halves,
   toasted
300g (10oz) mixed
   salad leaves (chicory,
   rocket and watercress
   work well)

FOR THE DRESSING

1 tbsp wholegrain mustard
1 tbsp Dijon mustard
2 tbsp white wine vinegar
2 tbsp runny honey
1 garlic clove
Juice of ½ lemon
Pinch of salt and pepper
120ml (4¼fl oz) extra
   virgin olive oil
   or walnut oil

METHOD

§   Place all the dressing ingredients, apart from the oil, into a food processor and blitz into a paste. Then, keeping the motor running, slowly add the oil in a thin but steady drizzle until all incorporated, and a thick emulsion has formed. Transfer to a suitable container and set aside.

§   Gently toss all the salad ingredients together in a large bowl. Lightly toss the salad with the dressing and serve immediately.

MUSHROOM AND CHESTNUT RISOTTO

Risotto rice must be one of the most useful back-ups in any pantry. Cooked with butter, vegetable oil (not olive), onions and garlic, you have the beginning of many supper dishes. The creaminess of the mushrooms absorbs very well into the rice but this is one dish you need to stand and stir, as that helps the rice – you cannot abandon risotto. It is, however, a favourite supper dish that I cook as friends stand around the Aga with me enjoying a glass of wine (which is what the risotto needs as well!).

PREPARATION TIME 15 mins   COOKING TIME 35 mins   SERVES 4–6

INGREDIENTS

30g (1¼oz) dried porcini mushrooms

2 tbsp olive oil

250g (9oz) fresh mushrooms (the more interesting the better), sliced

75g (3oz) butter, plus a little extra to finish

1 onion, finely chopped

2 garlic cloves, finely grated

400g (14oz) risotto rice (Arborio or Carnaroli are best)

250ml (9fl oz) white wine

1 litre (1¾ pints) warm stock (vegetable or chicken, whichever you prefer)

100g (3½oz) chestnuts, peeled and roughly chopped

1tsp olive oil

40g (1½oz) Parmesan, grated

Salt and pepper

Basil leaves, or chopped parsley, to serve

METHOD

§ Soak the dried porcini in a little bowl of boiling water for 10 minutes.

§ Drain the porcini, reserving the liquid but being mindful that grit can collect at the bottom of the bowl. Roughly chop the porcini and keep to one side, then add the reserved soaking liquid to the stock.

§ Heat the olive oil in a large casserole and when it is hot, fry the fresh mushrooms until they are just beginning to soften. Remove and keep to one side.

§ Add 25g (1oz) of the butter to the same pan and add the onion. Sweat for 5 minutes until softened, then add the garlic and cook for another minute.

§ Add the rice and stir so that each rice grain is coated with the butter and cook for a couple of minutes.

§ Pour the wine into the pan – it will hiss and quickly evaporate, releasing a wonderful smell and flavour. Then add a ladleful of stock and stir. Continue cooking, adding the stock one ladle at a time – you want the rice to have moisture available so that it can cook and expand, but not be too soupy. Stir gently to ensure that all the rice is evenly cooked.

§ When the rice is almost cooked, add in all the mushrooms and season to taste.

§ Meanwhile, melt another 25g (1oz) of the butter in a frying pan with the olive oil and fry the chestnuts until they are lightly browned.

§ When the rice is cooked to al dente, turn off the heat and add the last 25g (1oz) of butter. Add the chestnuts and stir through to distribute evenly.

§ I like to add the grated Parmesan and stir it well into the risotto, but equally, given this risotto has mushrooms and chestnuts, you could just sprinkle it over.

§ Put a little fresh basil or parsley on the top of each plate for colour as well as taste.

LADY CARNARVON'S SHEPHERD'S PIE

Saturday lunch, which may include my nieces and nephews (aged from two to nine years old), calls for unfussy family cooking, and shepherd's pie is a favourite. I therefore tend not to include garlic or celery in this, just carrots and peas. My mother scattered the potato topping with grated cheese, which I think is delicious, and everybody usually asks for ketchup.

This recipe will serve six hungry adults, or four adults and four children. Castle lunches tend to be larger and Paul, our chef, may well double the quantities, preparing this in at least two separate dishes. Lunch is therefore served promptly with guests on each side of the Dining Room table helping themselves as the dishes are taken round.

PREPARATION TIME **15 mins** COOKING TIME **1 hr 30 mins** SERVES **6**

INGREDIENTS

1 tbsp Highclere rapeseed oil

20g (¾oz) butter

1 large red onion, chopped

3 medium carrots, diced

800g (1¾lb) lamb mince

350ml (12fl oz) good lamb or beef stock (to which I usually add 2 tsp redcurrant jelly)

2 tbsp Worcestershire sauce

50g (2oz) tomato purée

2–3 sprigs of thyme

175g (6oz) frozen peas, thawed

10 mint leaves, finely chopped (optional)

FOR THE MASHED POTATO

1·5kg (3¼lb) potatoes (best floury or fluffy varieties such as Maris Piper or King Edward), peeled and chopped

100g (3½oz) butter

50–100ml (2–3½fl oz) milk

100g (3½oz) mature Cheddar, grated (optional)

Salt and pepper

METHOD

§   Preheat the oven to 200°C/400°F/Gas mark 6.

§   Heat the oil and butter in a large saucepan over a low heat.

§   Add the onion and carrots and cook for 8–10 minutes until softened. Add the lamb mince and cook for 5–6 minutes, stirring often to make sure it all browns, then add the stock and Worcestershire sauce and cook for 5 minutes.

§   Add the tomato purée and the thyme and let the mixture simmer gently for 30 minutes, stirring occasionally.

§   Meanwhile, put the potatoes into a pan of cold water and add a pinch of salt. Bring to the boil, lower the heat and let them bubble until they are soft, which should take 15–20 minutes. Drain and mash the potatoes with the butter and grind in some pepper. Add milk, but not so much that they become too soft – they need to sit on top of the meat, not sink into it. Keep to one side until you are ready to use them.

§   Add the peas to the lamb, along with the mint leaves if you are using them. Stir well to combine before tipping the lamb mixture into a roasting dish.

§   Spoon the potato evenly over the dish, then take a fork and drag it around to make tramlines which will add crispiness to the topping.

§   Bake for 30 minutes in the oven until the top crisps.

§   If you are using the cheese, remove the dish from the oven after 30 minutes, then scatter over the grated cheese and return the pie to the oven for another 5 minutes, or until the cheese is golden and melted.

§   Serve with broccoli, roasted root vegetables and ketchup.

The key is to use a really good dark meat stock, and the best one is undoubtedly made by our chef, Paul Brooke-Taylor. The fallback is a good organic stock cube mixed with consommé.

Cooking should be fun and to your taste – I might add some wine to the mince if I am cooking for a weekday supper, or I really like mixing some mashed celeriac into the potato to put on top, but I wholly understand either route may cause problems where children's taste is concerned!

Most importantly, shepherd's pie must be tasty. This version includes a red onion, which is packed with nutrients, as well as carrots and peas. I often add redcurrant jelly or quince jelly to stocks and gravies to give a little sweetness.

TURKEY RISSOLES WITH TOMATO SALSA

These are a splendid way to use up leftover turkey and are a great favourite of my husband Geordie. We sometimes serve with chutney instead of the salsa, or sometimes opt for a fried egg on top.

PREPARATION TIME **25 mins**   COOKING TIME **20 mins**   SERVES **4**

INGREDIENTS

FOR THE SALSA

4 large tomatoes, finely chopped

1 small red onion, very finely chopped

1 large garlic clove, crushed

Juice of ½ lime

100g (3½oz) coriander, chopped

A splash of red wine vinegar

FOR THE RISSOLES

500g (1lb 2oz) cooked turkey (leg and breast meat), finely chopped

1 small onion, very finely chopped

2 garlic cloves, crushed to a paste

1 tbsp rosemary leaves, finely chopped

50g (2oz) fresh breadcrumbs

1 egg, beaten

Rapeseed oil, for frying

Salt and pepper

METHOD

§   First make the salsa. Combine all the ingredients in a bowl.

§   To make the rissoles, place the turkey, onion, garlic, rosemary, breadcrumbs and egg in a mixing bowl and season with salt and pepper. Use your hands to mix well. Divide the mixture into eight equal portions and shape into patties, squeezing it all together.

§   Heat the oil over a medium heat in a frying pan and cook four rissoles at a time for 4–5 minutes on each side or until browned.

§   Remove from the pan and keep warm while you cook the remaining rissoles.

§   Serve with salsa and a crisp, green salad.

BEEF FILLET WELLINGTON

It is a New Year, so why not look forward and begin it with a treat? This is an extravagant and legendary dish. Like other flag-waving Britons, I rather assumed it derived from various preferences of the nineteenth-century Duke of Wellington, but it is only in 1939 in the *New York Food Guide* that this dish is described as 'Tenderloin of Beef Wellington'.

The French name for this dish is *filet de bœuf en croûte*, which could be stretched to suggest a hard outer covering allied to a wellington boot.

We are all likely to have had a good walk in boots before returning for an excellent lunch of this. I think this beef is good served with green beans, peas and cauliflower cheese and a good red wine – a Merlot such as Saint-Emilion or Pomerol – to toast the New Year.

PREPARATION TIME 30 mins   COOKING TIME 1 hour   SERVES 6–8

INGREDIENTS

800g (1¾lb) wild mushrooms, cleaned and finely chopped

4 banana shallots, finely diced

5 garlic cloves, finely grated

5 sprigs of thyme, leaves picked

20g (¾oz) unsalted butter

1 tbsp olive oil

1kg (2¼lb) fillet of beef, trimmed

100ml (3½fl oz) Madeira

8 slices of Parma ham

500g (1lb 2 oz) block of puff pastry

Flour, for dusting

1 egg, beaten

Salt and pepper

METHOD

§   Add the mushrooms, banana shallots, garlic and thyme leaves to a large bowl and mix. Set to one side – this is the duxelle.

§   Heat the butter and oil in a large frying pan over a medium heat until hot. Season the beef fillet with salt and pepper (but go lightly on the salt as the Parma ham will infuse its salty flavours during cooking) and place the meat in the hot pan.

§   Seal the fillet on all sides before removing to a plate to rest and cool.

§   Add the duxelle mix to the same pan to capture the beef flavours and return it to a high heat. Add the Madeira and cook until all the liquid has evaporated – the duxelle will become dark and dry out. When cooked, remove the duxelle from the pan and allow to cool.

§   On a clean worktop, lay out a large double layer rectangle of cling film – it needs to be twice the size of the beef fillet.

§   On top of this, lay out the Parma ham slices, slightly overlapping, again in a rectangle shape larger than the beef. Spread the duxelle over the Parma ham in a thin but even layer. Place the fillet of beef on the duxelle, and use the cling film to start to tightly wrap the Parma ham and duxelle mix around the sealed beef fillet, then twist the ends tightly to secure and put the meat into the fridge for a good hour to rest and set.

§   Preheat the oven to 200°C/400°F/Gas mark 6.

§   To assemble the Wellington, roll out the puff pastry on a lightly floured worktop, to approximately the thickness of a pound coin. Remove the cling film from the beef and place the beef onto the middle of the pastry. Fold up the two sides of the pastry and seal the edges with a little beaten egg. If you have a lot of overlap, trim the pastry so it overlaps by just 2cm (¾ inch).

§   Turn the beef so the join is underneath and tuck in the ends of the pastry to fully enclose it.

§   Carefully lift the Wellington onto a baking sheet lined with greaseproof paper and use the rest of the beaten egg to glaze the pastry.

§   Place the Wellington into the oven for 40–45 minutes, until golden brown.

§   Rest for 20 minutes before carving.

POACHED PEARS IN RED WINE

This particular pudding dates from my years at university (I went to St Andrews) and was one that my flatmate Smiles (her real name was Susannah) taught me. It looks very pretty and as usual can be prepared ahead which would leave me plenty of time to get ready for a party!

Paul, our chef here at Highclere, has added a cartouche (a paper covering to stop a skin forming on top of the liquid) but I was never and am still not quite so perfect in my finish! Use a good fruit red wine such as a Beaujolais; you neither want an insipid one nor one with too much tannin.

I used to serve the pears with a dollop of thick Greek yoghurt.

PREPARATION TIME **20 mins**   COOKING TIME **40 mins**   SERVES **8**

INGREDIENTS

8 pears
2 bottles of red wine
300g (10½oz) brown sugar
1 cinnamon stick
4 star anise
4 bay leaf
1 vanilla pod,
   split and scraped

METHOD

§   Peel the pears and trim the bottoms so the pears stand upright.

§   Stand the pears in a heavy-based pan, and cover with the red wine, then add the sugar, cinnamon stick, star anise, bay leaf and vanilla pod, then cover the pears with a cartouche. If the liquid doesn't quite cover, just top up with a little water.

§   Gently bring to a simmer and cook for around 30 minutes until just soft, then turn off the heat and allow the pears to cool in the wine. Remove the pears from the stock and boil the remaining stock to reduce it to a sticky syrup.

§   Plate the pears and spoon over the reduced syrup.

SPICED NUTS

Nuts have so many health properties, there is little need to confirm what a positive role they play. One reason why Highclere has been settled and farmed for so many centuries is because the hazels and walnuts grew so well here over good, clean chalk water.

An amusing story about nuts comes from the end of World War Two (December 1944), when four German couriers approached American lines under a flag of truce, carrying a message 'from the German Commander to the American Commander.'

Asserting that Bastogne was 'encircled', the note gave McAuliffe, who was acting commander of the 101st, two hours to surrender. General Mac read the note and said, 'Aw, nuts.' Then he asked, 'What should I tell them?'

Lt. Col. Harry W.O. Kinnard, the division operations officer, said, 'Why not tell them what you just said?' McAuliffe then scribbled a reply: 'To the German commander: Nuts! From the American commander.'

PREPARATION TIME 5 mins   COOKING TIME 15 mins

INGREDIENTS

500g (1lb 2oz) unsalted mixed nuts (whole almonds, cashews, hazelnuts and walnuts – or whichever you like)

2 tbsp rosemary, chopped

½ tsp cayenne pepper

2 tsp dark brown sugar

2 tsp sea salt

1 tbsp unsalted butter, melted

METHOD

§   Preheat the oven to 180°C/350°F/Gas mark 4.

§   Mix the nuts to combine and spread them out on a baking sheet. Toast in the oven for 10–15 minutes, turning them halfway through, until they become light golden brown.

§   In a large bowl, combine the rosemary, cayenne pepper, sugar, salt and melted butter.

§   Thoroughly toss the toasted nuts with the spiced butter to coat. Serve warm.

HIGHCLERE CASTLE BULLSHOT

The television series *Jeeves and Wooster*, starring Stephen Fry and Hugh Laurie, was filmed here at Highclere Castle nearly thirty years ago. The series was adapted from a wonderful series of books by P.G. Wodehouse that were set during the late 1920s and 1930s and told tales of the charming and slightly hopeless Bertie Wooster, who is looked after by his highly intelligent valet, Jeeves.

Jeeves quite often had to rectify Bertie's hangovers and employed a kind of magic potion – in fact a species of Bullshot:

> *It is the Worcester sauce that gives it its colour. The raw egg makes it nutritious. The red pepper gives it its bite. Gentlemen have told me they have found it extremely invigorating after a late evening.*

A Bullshot is an uplifting and reviving drink which is often forgotten about – and it does not require you to have a hangover beforehand. You can serve this cold or hot.

PREPARATION TIME 5 mins   COOKING TIME 5 mins   SERVES 6

INGREDIENTS

500ml (18fl oz) tomato juice

500ml (18fl oz) beef consommé or stock

Generous splash of Worcestershire sauce

Careful splash of Tabasco, to taste

Juice of 1 lemon

200–300ml (7–10½fl oz) vodka, to taste

½ tsp celery salt

Celery stalks, to garnish

Ice, if serving cold

METHOD

TO SERVE COLD

§   Combine the tomato juice, beef stock, Worcestershire sauce, Tabasco, lemon juice and vodka in a jug, mix well and season with celery salt.

§   Pour into glasses over ice, add a celery stalk and serve.

TO SERVE WARM

§   Combine the tomato juice, beef stock, Worcestershire sauce, Tabasco and lemon juice in a saucepan and heat until almost at a simmer.

§   Remove from the heat and add the vodka, season with celery salt, pour into mugs and serve with a celery stalk.

CHAPTER TWELVE

EPIPHANY & AFTER

🌿 TWELFTH NIGHT FALLS 🌿

ON 6 JANUARY — OFFICIALLY SPEAKING,

IT IS THE CHRISTIAN FEAST DAY OF EPIPHANY, celebrating the revelation of God incarnate as Jesus Christ. In the West, it is celebrated as the day on which the three Kings, or Magi, arrived with their gifts for the baby Jesus, but the Eastern churches celebrate it more for Jesus' baptism in the River Jordan. It also marks the end of King Alfred's original official Christmas holiday and remains a national holiday in many parts of Europe, though sadly not in England.

BY TRADITION ALL THE CHRISTMAS DECORATIONS AND the trees should come down on Twelfth Night, 6 January, otherwise folklore says you risk bad luck. If you don't take them down, the only way out then, according to tradition, is to keep them up all the way to Candlemas, on 2 February, by which time, I suspect, the tree at least would be in something of a parlous state.

Packing away the Christmas decorations is a rather anti-climactic, painstaking and somewhat prickly job, given the pine needles. Judging by Diana's face, it is also something of a relief as it is impossible to deny the steady fall of needles and tired dry branches. The gardeners and banqueting team return again to dismantle the tree and Sally from the gift shop reappears to organise the process as the lights are carefully taken down and the different-coloured baubles are sorted, packed away in old newspaper, labelled and stored again on the top floor of the Castle. The tree is cut up in situ; first the lower branches are sawn off, then it is carefully lowered onto sheeting, the trunk cut into manageable lengths and the whole lot carried out.

Elsewhere in the Castle, the Christmas cards are gathered up to be taken to my office so that new addresses or other vital information in them can be noted down, the wreaths dismantled and the once-fresh greenery can be composted. The stair garlands are carefully taken down and coiled into boxes whilst the other smaller trees and decorations are removed. The gardeners continue their work outside as the courtyard and driveway trees are denuded of decorations and lights and also carted away. It is almost as if the whole Castle gives itself a shake, readying itself for the new year ahead.

Inside, Diana and her team set to work to sweep, hoover and finally bring out the buffing machine to restore the floors. The carpets are put back and the furniture, moved to make way for the decorations, is returned in its more usual positions. To my mind, the Castle suddenly looks very bare without all the colour and sparkle and I ask the gardeners to put out great bowls of cyclamen for their vibrant colour and pots of paperwhite narcissi for their wonderful spring scent, which mixes so evocatively with the smell of the furniture wax.

EPIPHANIES ARE, IN ALL THEIR MEANINGS, MOST HELPFUL, and I am personally always very happy when I have one – that sudden intuitive insight, the illuminating moment. The etymology of the word itself pre-dates Christianity; Greek in origin, it suggests showing of light as opposed to darkness, and thus is associated with the appearance of dawn.

In past times, the eve of Twelfth Night was one of celebration and as large a party as Christmas Day itself. The drinks served on this occasion were often hot and spicy, recalling the spices brought by the Magi, with heavily fruited Twelfth Night cakes and Epiphany tarts, with the pastry laid out in the shape of the star of Bethlehem. The yule log was finally put

out during the evening after wassails, mumming and, often, practical jokes. It was a night of revelry and the last day in power of the Lord of Misrule before the natural order of command reasserted itself. Perhaps the last vestige of this ancient tradition of 'misrule' is the modern-day pantomime, a traditional Christmas theatre play where authority always is mocked, the hero is played by a woman and the leading older female character, the dame, is played by a man.

Sumptuous Epiphany celebrations were above all a feature of Tudor times, from Henry VII celebrating mass before a feast, to Henry VIII who loved 'disguisings' – he would celebrate Twelfth Night magnificently with a banquet, games and the staging of plays. Traditions continued through the time of Elizabeth I whilst, outside the Court, Mystery Plays were staged and processions wound their way through towns to illustrate the story and legend.

Despite its disappearance from the modern calendar, in this country at least, Twelfth Night is still part of our memory because of the William Shakespeare play of the same name. First performed on the eve of Epiphany in 1601, this comedy relies on confusion and mistaken identity, taking the theme from these twelve days of 'misrule' in which servants often dressed up as their masters, men as women, and so forth, casting the normal order into confusion. Utterly embedded in the language and touchstones of his time, Shakespeare's lines highlight the underlying themes of *Twelfth Night*:

'I say there is no darkness but ignorance,' (The Fool). Just as Epiphany welcomes the dawn and the light, so in the same way the final scenes of the play allow the world to return to order, although the sense that 'Nothing that is so, is so' stays with the audience.

Samuel Pepys, however, was not so enamoured of the play and wrote in his diary that he 'saw *Twelfth Night* acted well, though it be but a silly play, and not related at all to the name or day'. Following the restoration of the monarchy with Charles II in 1660, the feast of Epiphany slowly came to be reinstated and, again referring to Pepys's diaries from 6 January (1668):

> These were my guests, and Mrs. Turner's friend, whom I saw the other day, Mr. Wicken, and very merry we were at dinner, and so all the afternoon, talking, and looking up and down my house; and in the evening I did bring out my cake – a noble cake, and there cut it into pieces, with wine and good drink: and after a new fashion, to prevent spoiling the cake, did put so many titles into a hat, and so drew cuts; and I was the Queene; and The Turner, King – Creed, Sir Martin Marrall; and Betty, Mrs. Millicent: and so we were mighty merry till it was night; and then, being moonshine and fine frost, they went home, I lending some of them my coach to help to carry them, and so my wife and I spent the rest of the evening in talk and reading, and so with great pleasure to bed.

One hundred and eighty years later, Charles Dickens, unique among novelists at that time in his enthusiastic public performances, celebrated Twelfth Night throughout his life with pageantry, games, forfeits, charades and genial merriment.

During Queen Victoria's reign, since it was not a public holiday, the approach became increasingly decorous and the feasting and drinking became more modest, even if the reversal of roles was still played out in drawing rooms. The Royal Household celebrated Twelfth Night with an enormous and elaborate Epiphany cake decorated with figures and dancers, whilst carols such as 'As with gladness, men of old, Did the guiding star behold' or 'We three Kings of Orient Are' were sung in preference to the ribaldry of earlier times.

IN GREECE, EPIPHANY IS CALLED THEOPHANY, LITERALLY 'the manifestation of a deity to a worshipper', and is marked with feasts and traditional foods. So-called 'King Cakes' are found in various forms in many countries. In Malta they are honeyed rings, whilst in France you might eat a Galette des Rois – a flat almond cake decorated with a gold paper crown.

In 2011, an Act of Parliament restored Epiphany as an official, non-working, national public holiday in Poland. There, 'Three Kings' cakes' are

These days no one expects a lavish feast on Twelfth Night, but a comforting supper will lift spirits after packing away the decorations:

FISH PIE
PAGE 304

APPLE CHARLOTTE
PAGE 306

Try the recipe we use
at the Castle for our
EPIPHANY TART
which children will
enjoy helping to make
PAGE 311

served with a coin or a whole almond baked inside, and whoever gets it becomes king or queen for the day, signified by wearing the paper crown that decorates the cake. According to Polish tradition this person will be lucky in the coming year.

Other variations of King Cake in different places include: a golden pastry ring filled with orange and spice to represent the gold, frankincense and myrrh; a construction of seven large buns, stacked into a crown and studded with citron; a rich, fruited bread dough flavoured with cardamom and shaped into a crown. And in Louisiana, where Epiphany marks the start of the Carnival, round cakes are filled with cinnamon and decorated with white icing sprinkled with brightly coloured sugars.

AFTER THE CELEBRATIONS OF EPIPHANY, THE FOLLOWING Monday it was back to work. This was the official end of the Twelve Days of Christmas and often called Plough Monday as, traditionally, this was when agricultural workers resumed their duties in the fields after the Christmas break. In some villages it was celebrated with a procession. A plough attached to long ropes was drawn by up to forty men in clean white shirts with brightly coloured ribbons tied to their arms, shoulders and hats. Musicians, and sometimes Morris Men, joined the celebrations, with a fool collecting money from spectators to spend on a convivial night in the local alehouse. A lack of donations towards the convivial enterprise could lead to your front garden being ploughed up.

Lacking the agricultural imperatives and connections with countryside and season in our lives, we often seem to return to work too soon after Christmas or New Year, where we are then persuaded that abstinence and austerity is the course forwards as a sort of punishment for our jollity. I cannot help feeling that this is a significant contributor to the sense of flatness and lack of energy that so dominates early January.

C A N D L E M A S
2 F E B R U A R Y

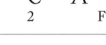

FORTY DAYS AFTER CHRISTMAS DAY COMES CANDLEMAS. Officially it marks the ritual presentation of the baby Jesus to God, but it is also the celebration of light. It was on this day that all the Church's candles were blessed for the following year. Today, in most countries, we take electric lights for granted, yet they have only been in our homes for such a short time, perhaps 150 years at most. Dame Maggie Smith, of course, as the Dowager Lady Grantham in *Downton Abbey*, marked their arrival with the comment, 'Such a glare', shading her eyes with her fan, and Geordie's grandfather would famously declare that all the lights were to be turned off immediately after dinner to save electricity. Robert the Butler would

then arrive bearing an array of torches on a silver tray in order for the guests to be able to find their way upstairs to bed.

It is easy to forget the importance and value of candles and the very real difference between light and dark. In 2019, candles are a wonderful treat, throwing flickering lights, often accompanied by soothing scents, and leaving flattering shadows around rooms and faces. In pre-Christian times, 2 February was the festival of light because it was the mid-point of winter, halfway between the winter solstice (shortest day) and the spring equinox. Thus on Candlemas many people placed lighted candles in their windows to scare away evil spirits that may have been present on the dark winter nights.

There are other superstitions associated with this day as well. Being British, the best-known one is about the weather:

If Candlemas Day be fair and bright
Winter will have another fight.
If Candlemas Day brings cloud and rain,
Winter won't come again.

Apparently, if someone brings snowdrops into the house on Candlemas Day it symbolises a parting or death. I am not exactly sure how this superstition works as snowdrops were once called Candlemas bells and, as a symbol of purity and light, they were brought into churches on this day.

ABOVE
Highclere's chapel
and graveyard

300

In older churchyards you will still find drifts of snowdrops planted to supply flowers for Candlemas. We have planted some here in the park and they nestle amongst the curled-up brown leaves like tiny white lanterns. Despite their delicacy, they appear with fortitude during the harshest month of the year. Their thin, long green leaves have specially hardened tips which help them break through the frozen earth, whilst their sap contains a form of antifreeze to prevent ice crystals forming. They are a sight to behold and a promise that the days will soon be lengthening and spring is not too far away. I wonder sometimes if we have forgotten to find such thoughts amongst the natural world around us – more of us now live in towns rather than the rural countryside and we forget what to look for. Yet without understanding and enjoying nature, I do not think we live so well.

Christmas these days is celebrated by both Christians and non-Christians, and as such is both a cultural and a religious event. The celebration of winter, of the feasts, of family, the hope for the New Year, of folklore, legend and entertainment gathers us all together. It reminds us of childhood, of memories and absent friends and of passing years, and when it is over, we have the promise of spring, of snowdrops, of swallows, of cherry blossom and the emerging crops and newborn lambs to look forward to.

HAM HOCK TERRINE

This is a spectacular looking and very tasty dish that makes a wonderful starter for a formal feast. If any is left over, then the following day's lunch or supper is the work of a moment.

PREPARATION TIME 30 mins   COOKING TIME 4 hours, plus cooling and chilling overnight
MAKES 10–12 portions

INGREDIENTS

4 'green' ham hocks
    (cured but unsmoked)
6 bay leaves
15 black peppercorns
6 star anise
1 cinnamon stick
6 sprigs of rosemary
1 bunch of thyme
75g (3oz) demerara sugar
    per kg of ham hock
40g (1½oz) curly parsley,
    chopped
1 tbsp English mustard
Zest and juice
    of 2 large oranges
Salt and pepper

METHOD

§   Rinse the hocks under cold running water for a good 5 minutes, then place them in a large saucepan or stockpot and cover with fresh water. Add the bay leaves, peppercorns, star anise, cinnamon stick, rosemary and thyme. Then add the weighed sugar. Bring to the boil then turn down to a simmer and cook for 3½ hours, or until the meat is falling from the bone. You will need to keep skimming the surface of the water for scum and other impurities that rise up. Top up the pot with cold water as it evaporates – this will also help the fat rise for skimming.

§   Remove from the heat and allow the hocks to cool in the pan for an hour.

§   Very carefully remove the meat from the stock with a slotted spoon and set aside. Pass the stock through a fine sieve, discarding all the solids, and place the stock back on to boil to reduce.

§   Pick the meat off the bones and gently break it up with your hands. You are after lovely flakes and chunks of meat. Place these in a mixing bowl and season with salt and pepper to taste. Add the parsley, English mustard and a little orange zest and juice.

§   Add one ladleful of the reduced stock to the meat, stir, then transfer to a 1·5 litre (2½ pint) terrine mould lined with cling film, and press down firmly.

§   Cover with cling film and weight the top. Place in the fridge to chill overnight. It will set in its own gelatine and be ready to slice.

§   This is delicious served with a dressed green salad and, if you can get it, mostarda – a northern Italian condiment made of candied fruit and a mustard-flavoured syrup (shown in the photo). If you are lucky someone may give you a jar for Christmas!

FISH PIE

Britain is an island surrounded by good cold waters with diverse fish. Few excuses are needed to produce a fish pie, and if I can I will make one on a Friday, as in former, more religious days, that was the day on which we avoided eating meat. My mother used to make a delicious fish pie that included sliced hard-boiled eggs and I can well remember watching her make the béchamel sauce.

PREPARATION TIME 15 mins COOKING TIME 1 hr 15 mins, plus cooling SERVES 8

INGREDIENTS

800g (1¾lb) mixed fresh fish (salmon, cod, haddock, trout – up to you)

500g (1lb 2oz) shellfish (lobster, prawns, scallops – again, up to you)

3 bay leaves

10 black peppercorns

2 banana shallots, cut in half

1 litre (1¾ pints) milk

4 eggs (optional)

2kg (4½lb) red-skinned potatoes, or Maris Piper, peeled and chopped

250g (9oz) butter

100g (3½oz) plain flour

Freshly grated nutmeg

20g (¾oz) parsley, finely chopped

A mugful of vintage Cheddar cheese, grated (optional)

Salt and pepper

METHOD

§   Preheat the oven to 170°C/325°F/Gas mark 3.

§   Lay the fish and shellfish in a large sauté pan, add the bay leaves, peppercorns and shallot halves and pour over the milk. Bring the milk up to a simmer, then turn off the heat and allow the fish to poach in the residual heat for around 10 minutes.

§   When cool enough to handle, carefully lift the fish from the milk and place in a dish. Strain the milk into a jug and reserve to make the béchamel sauce.

§   If you are adding the eggs, boil them for about 8 minutes, then run them under cold water immediately to stop them cooking, and leave until cool enough to handle. Peel and cut each one in half.

§   Add the potatoes to a pan of cold water, with a good pinch of salt, and place over a high heat to bring to the boil. Cook for 15–20 minutes until cooked through, then drain into a colander before returning to the pan. Mash the potatoes with 150g (5oz) of the butter and plenty of freshly ground pepper.

§   To make the béchamel sauce, melt the remaining 100g (3½oz) butter in a heavy-based pan along with the flour, and stirring with a wooden spoon, cook for 3 minutes over a medium heat. Slowly start to add the reserved milk, a little at a time, stirring as you go with the wooden spoon. Once it is all poured in, stir well over a low heat to get rid of any lumps in the sauce.

§   Season to taste and sprinkle over some grated nutmeg. Remove from the heat.

§   Carefully flake the fish into the pan in big pieces, removing any bones as you go.

§   Add the chopped parsley and gently stir to coat the fish before transferring to a large ovenproof dish and levelling it out. Press the egg halves down into the fish mix, if using.

§   Spoon the potato evenly over the dish, then take a fork and drag it around to make tramlines, which will add crispiness to the topping. (If you are feeling ambitious you can pipe it in small rosettes, as shown in the picture.) Bake for 30 minutes in the oven until the top crisps and it is golden and bubbling.

§   If you are using the cheese, remove the dish from the oven after 30 minutes and scatter over the grated cheese, then return the pie to the oven for another 5 minutes, or until the cheese is melted.

§   Check it is piping hot before serving with fresh green vegetables or a green salad.

APPLE CHARLOTTE
WITH CINNAMON CREAM

This pudding is a favourite with the family and is named after Queen Charlotte, wife of King George III.

PREPARATION TIME 15 mins, plus resting   COOKING TIME 1 hour   SERVES 4–6

INGREDIENTS

450g (1lb) apples
  (half Bramley [cooking]
  and half Cox [eating] if
  possible), peeled, cored
  and chopped
1 tbsp caster sugar
1 tsp ground cinnamon
120g (4¼oz) butter
6–8 slices of bread about
  5mm (¼ inch) thick,
  crusts removed
1 egg yolk

TO SERVE

Whipped cream
Ground cinnamon,
  icing sugar and vanilla
  essence, to taste

METHOD

§   Preheat the oven to 200°C/400°F/Gas mark 6.

§   Place the apples in a saucepan with the sugar, cinnamon and 30g (1oz) of the butter, place over a low heat and cook the apples until soft, which should take 10–15 minutes.

§   Melt the remaining butter and cut the bread into rectangles. Dip one side of the bread into the butter and line a 1 litre (1¾ pints) pudding basin, overlapping the slices, and press firmly into the mould, buttery side to the basin.

§   When the apple mixture is cooled, beat the egg yolk into it and fill the bread-lined pudding basin. Seal the top with the remaining buttered bread slices, butter facing you.

§   Place an ovenproof plate on top of the pudding with a suitable weight on top. Place to one side for 30 minutes. Put the pudding into the oven for 35 minutes, then carefully remove the plate from the top and continue to bake for 10 minutes until golden brown on top.

§   Remove from the oven, leave to rest in the basin for 10 minutes before turning out onto a warmed plate to serve.

§   Best served with softly whipped cream, flavoured to your taste by stirring through cinnamon, icing sugar and vanilla essence..

BETTY'S MARMALADE

Betty Gale was the housekeeper to Geordie's parents, the 7th Earl and Countess of Carnarvon. Her marmalade is sharper in taste and runnier than the usual variety but we all prefer it that way.

PREPARATION TIME 30 mins, plus soaking   COOKING TIME 2 hrs 15 mins   MAKES about 4·5kg (10lb)

INGREDIENTS

1·3kg (2¾lb)
  Seville oranges
2 lemons
3·5 litres (6 pints) water
2·7kg (6lb) preserving
  or granulated sugar

METHOD

§   Wash the fruit, cut in half and squeeze out the juice. Peel out the membranes and put these, with the pips, into a muslin bag.

§   Chop the peel to the desired thickness (we prefer finely chopped peel) and put in a large bowl with the juices, the pips bag and half of the water to soak overnight.

§   The next day, put everything into a pan with the rest of the water and simmer gently for about 2 hours until the liquid has reduced by half. Remove the muslin bag and squeeze it out well into the pan.

§   Add the sugar and stir over a low heat until it is all dissolved. Boil rapidly until you reach setting point –about 15 minutes. (Setting point is reached when the jam is at 104.5°C on a sugar thermometer, or when a little jam is dropped onto a cold plate and wrinkles when pressed with a finger.)

§   Leave to stand for at least half an hour to allow to settle. Pour into clean, dry, sterilised pots (see below) and seal.

TO STERILISE JARS

§   Wash them and their lids thoroughly in warm soapy water and rinse clean. Place directly on an oven shelf, making sure they are not touching each other (do not place washed rubber stoppers/seals in the oven). Heat the oven to 140°C/280°F/Gas mark 1½ and let the bottles or jars dry out for 15–20 minutes.

EPIPHANY TART

Traditionally, an Epiphany tart was made with thirteen different colours and types of jam to represent Jesus and his Twelve Apostles. These sit in a star-shaped pastry lattice which represents the star that led the Three Kings to find baby Jesus. It was considered a delicacy during Victorian times and cooks would compete to create intricate patterns that most closely resembled a stained-glass window. We use just three jams, but you can use whatever you have – preserves, lemon curd, marmalade – to provide a colourful contrasting pattern. Serve with a strong cup of tea on 6 January as part of your final Christmas celebrations.

PREPARATION TIME **20 mins, plus chilling**   COOKING TIME **35 mins**   SERVES 6

INGREDIENTS

100g (3½oz) soft butter, diced

75g (3oz) caster sugar

1 egg

200g (7oz) plain flour, plus extra for dusting

Pinch of salt

Dash of vanilla extract

3 or more different jams (raspberry, apricot and plum make a good contrast)

METHOD

§   Preheat the oven to 180°C/350°F/Gas mark 4.

§   Beat together the butter and sugar until fluffy and pale, then add the egg, flour, salt and vanilla and work the mixture until a smooth pastry is achieved.

§   Wrap in cling film and refrigerate for 20 minutes.

§   Warm the jams slightly so they will pour evenly into the pastry compartments when ready.

§   Roll out the pastry on a lightly floured surface to the thickness of a £1 coin, and line a lightly greased 25cm (10 inch) tart tin. We use a small ball of pastry to press the corners and edges into the case without breaking it.

§   Using the remaining pastry, construct 'ramparts' of pastry within the case, in the shape of a Star of David or 2 triangles, one inverted over the other. Line each compartment with tin foil and fill with baking beans.

§   Bake in the centre of the oven for 15 minutes, then remove the tin-foil sections and bake for a further 5 minutes.

§   Carefully pour the warmed jam into each compartment, using alternate colours to create a pattern.

§   Allow the jams to cool and set.

THANK YOU

I HAVE LOVED WRITING THIS BOOK. IT HAS BEEN a challenge and yet when I sent it off to Penguin Random House I felt it was complete. My agent, Ed Victor, who has sadly died, suggested I write a book about Christmas. I listened and thought about how to bring together the heart of the story, the traditions, and the cooking. It comes from my heart, from my memories and is for all of us to enjoy as we celebrate together. Thank you so much to everyone who has helped support me as I created and refined this book.

It brings together photographs from Chaz Oldham who explores the outside journeys and landscape and walked (thank you!) for miles through Highclere in pursuit of the photographs of land and woodland. Thank you so much to Paul Winch-Furness for the clarity of his food photography and for his calmness in moments of stress. Many thanks to Adam Hillier who has photographed the scenes of warmth and laughter, the detail, my nieces, dogs and Muffet the Shetland pony.

Thank you so much to Sally Popplewell and Justine Grace who edited and stayed with me into long evenings approaching the deadline, checking the details of recipe and text. David Rymill our admirable archivist read everything carefully and as ever I always value his thoughts and accurate suggestions.

Thank you to the Highclere Castle Kitchen team, led by Paul Brooke-Taylor, for delicious food, accurate recipes and for their enthusiasm and team spirit. Luis and the banqueting team remained undaunted by re-setting tables, making ever more cocktails and aiding and abetting Sally and her Christmas elf team.

Hannah Gutteridge helped style the photographs beautifully and Henrietta Gundill helped with our wreath making. Thank you both.

My sister Georgie and her children helped unwrap presents, run round corridors, hide under tables and ride Muffet – they are such fun to have for Christmas, thank you. Thank you to my friends and to Team Highclere for joining in with this project and I hope they all enjoy the book.

Thank you to Susan Sandon and her team at Penguin Random House, to Trevor Dolby and Tim Barnes for setting the book out with clarity and beauty, and to Charlie Brotherton who has helped me after Ed Victor's demise.

My beloved husband Geordie encouraged me as I took laptop and books on holidays, reading and remembering Christmas, acting as editor and photographer. My son Edward is always positive as my late writing hours extend and my deadline looms. Thank you both.

5 7 9 10 8 6 4

Century
20 Vauxhall Bridge Road
London SW1V 2SA

Century is part of the Penguin Random House
group of companies whose addresses can be found
at global.penguinrandomhouse.com.

Penguin
Random House
UK

First published by Century in 2019

www.penguin.co.uk

A CIP catalogue record for this book is available from the
British Library.

ISBN 978 1 8480 9522 9

Edited by Trevor Dolby

Designed by Tim Barnes, herechickychicky.com

Recipe testing by Kat Mead

Printed and bound by L.E.G.O. S.p.A.

Penguin Random House is committed to a sustainable
future for our business, our readers and our planet.

This book is made from Forest Stewardship Council®
certified paper.

FSC
www.fsc.org

MIX
Paper from
responsible sources
FSC® C016897